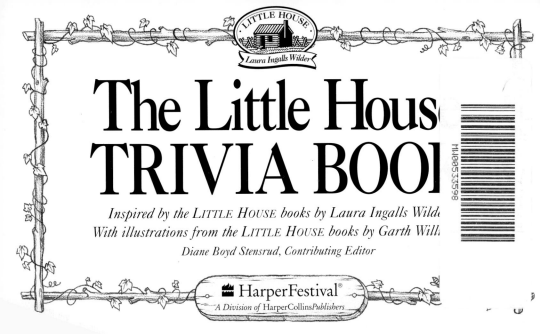

LITTLE HOUSE

Laura Ingalls Wilder

The Little House
TRIVIA BOOK

Inspired by the LITTLE HOUSE books by Laura Ingalls Wilder

With illustrations from the LITTLE HOUSE books by Garth Williams

Diane Boyd Stensrud, *Contributing Editor*

HarperFestival®
A Division of HarperCollins Publishers

The Little House Trivia Book
Copyright © 1996 by HarperCollins Publishers
Border art by Pat Schories. Designed by Alicia Mikles.
HarperFestival and Little House are registered trademarks of HarperCollins Publishers, Inc.
U.S. Reg. Nos. 1,781,351 and 1,771,442.
Printed in Hong Kong. All rights reserved.

THE LITTLE HOUSE TRIVIA BOOK

1. In what state is the little house in the Big Woods?

2. What color is the Ingallses' little house?

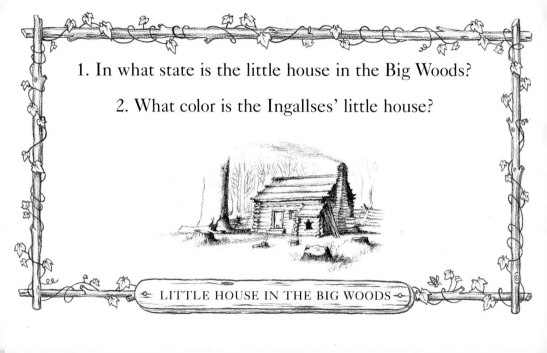

LITTLE HOUSE IN THE BIG WOODS

1. Wisconsin.

2. Gray.

Once upon a time . . . a little girl lived in the
Big Woods of Wisconsin, in a little gray house made of logs.

LITTLE HOUSE IN THE BIG WOODS

3. Where do Laura and Mary go
to play house during the winter?

4. What are Laura's two favorite days of the week?

LITTLE HOUSE IN THE BIG WOODS

3. *The attic.*

In the attic Laura and Mary
played house with the squashes and the pumpkins,
and everything was snug and cozy.

4. *Thursday and Saturday.*

Laura liked the churning and the baking days best of all the week.

LITTLE HOUSE IN THE BIG WOODS

5. What is Pa's nickname for Laura?

6. What does Ma give Laura for her birthday?

5. *"My little half-pint of cider half drunk up."*

6. *Five cakes.*

Ma gave her five little cakes, one for each
year that Laura had lived with her and Pa.

7. Why does Ma slap a bear?

8. What is the name of Pa's big green book?

7. Because she thinks the bear is Sukey the cow!

Then Laura said, "Ma, was it a bear?"

"Yes, Laura," Ma said. "It was a bear."

8. The Wonders of the Animal World.

9. Which dress of Ma's has a
pattern that looks like strawberries?

10. Who does Laura argue with at Grandma's house?

9. *The delaine dress.*

Ma's delaine dress was beautiful.
It was a dark green, with a little pattern all over it
that looked like ripe strawberries.

10. *Another Laura Ingalls!*

LITTLE HOUSE IN THE BIG WOODS

11. What does Ma use to curl Laura and Mary's hair before they go to town?

12. How many miles is town from the little house?

11. Rags.

She divided their long hair into wisps, combed each wisp with a wet comb
and wound it tightly on a bit of rag. . . . In the morning their hair would be curly.

12. Seven miles.

It was seven miles to town. The town was named Pepin,
and it was on the shore of Lake Pepin.

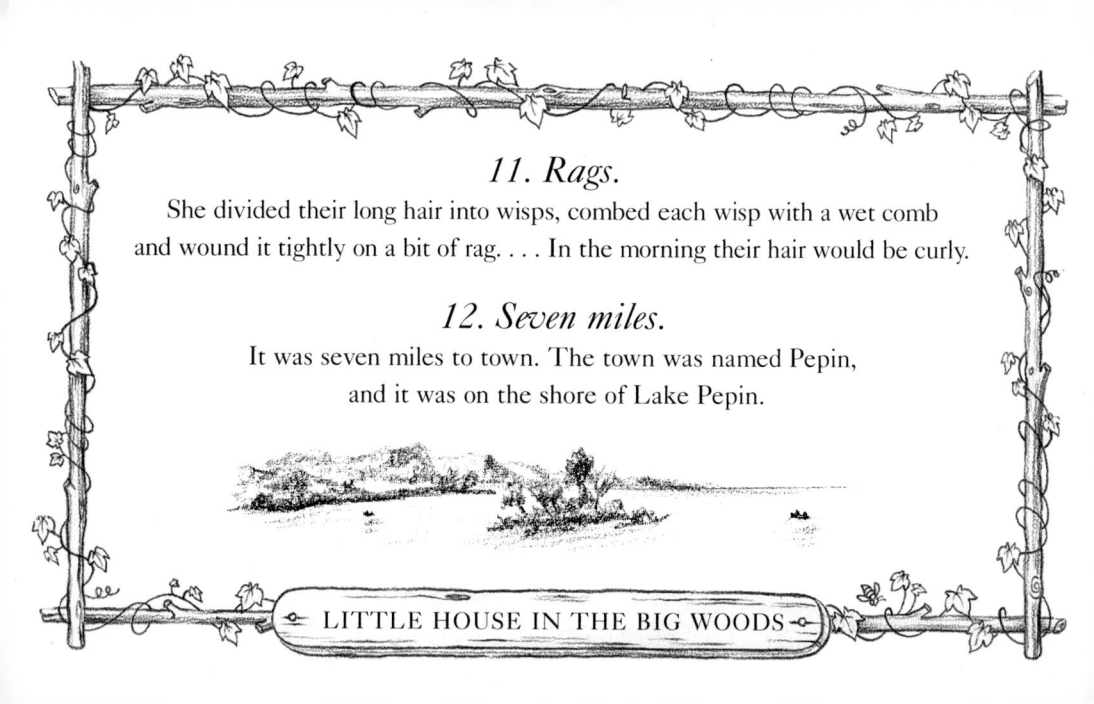

LITTLE HOUSE IN THE BIG WOODS

13. What does the printing on Laura's candy say?

14. What does the printing on Mary's candy say?

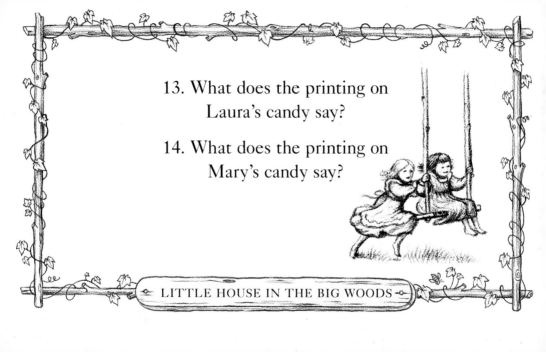

13. Sweets to the sweet.

14. Roses are red,
    Violets are blue,
    Sugar is sweet,
    And so are you.

LITTLE HOUSE IN THE BIG WOODS

15. Who is Clarence?

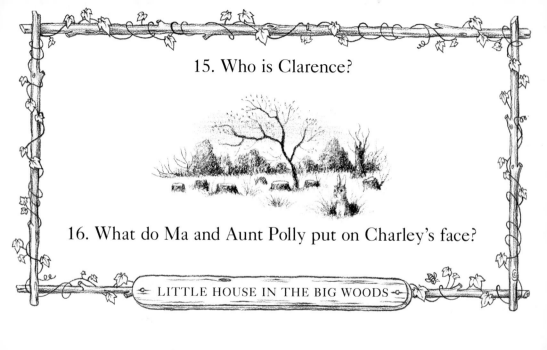

16. What do Ma and Aunt Polly put on Charley's face?

15. A neighbor Laura plays with.

Clarence was red-headed and freckled, and always laughing.

16. Mud.

Ma and Aunt Polly covered his whole face with mud
and tied the mud on with cloths.

17. What does Ma make with braided straws?

18. What is the "wonderful machine"?

LITTLE HOUSE IN THE BIG WOODS

17. *Straw hats.*

Ma could make beautiful hats. Laura liked to watch her,
and she learned how to braid the straw and make a little hat for Charlotte.

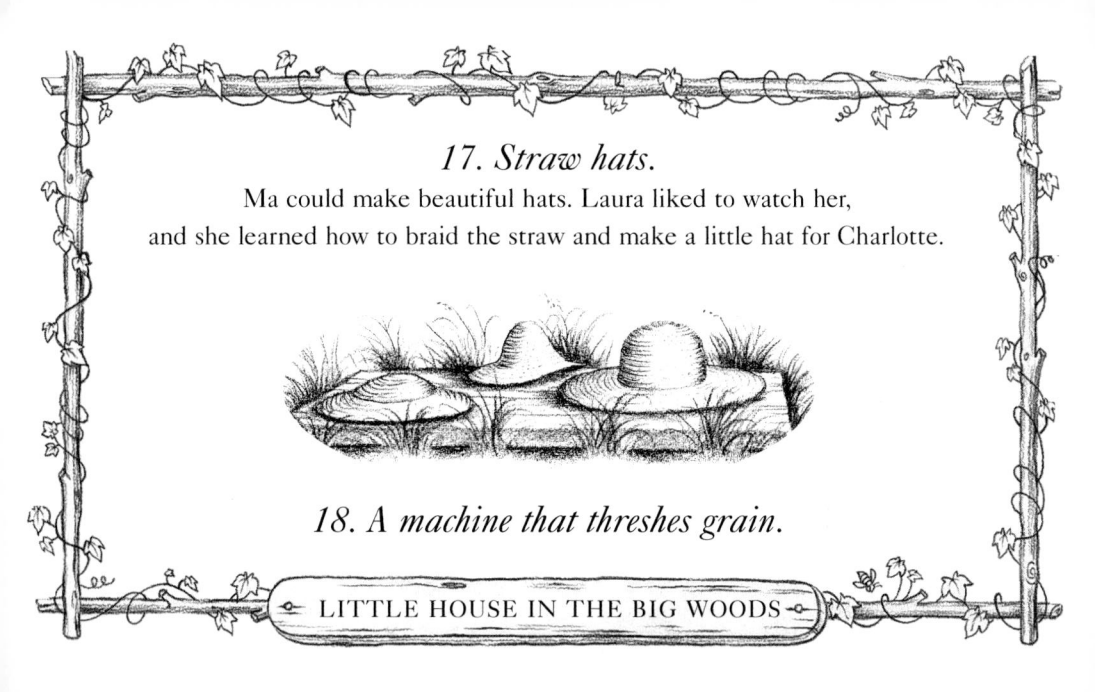

18. *A machine that threshes grain.*

1. What river do the Ingallses first cross
   when they leave the Big Woods?

2. What kind of horses are Pet and Patty?

LITTLE HOUSE ON THE PRAIRIE

1. The Mississippi.
Pa caught Laura up in his safe, big hug.
"We're across the Mississippi!" he said, hugging her joyously.

2. Western mustangs.
They were beautiful little horses, and Pa said they were not really ponies;
they were western mustangs.

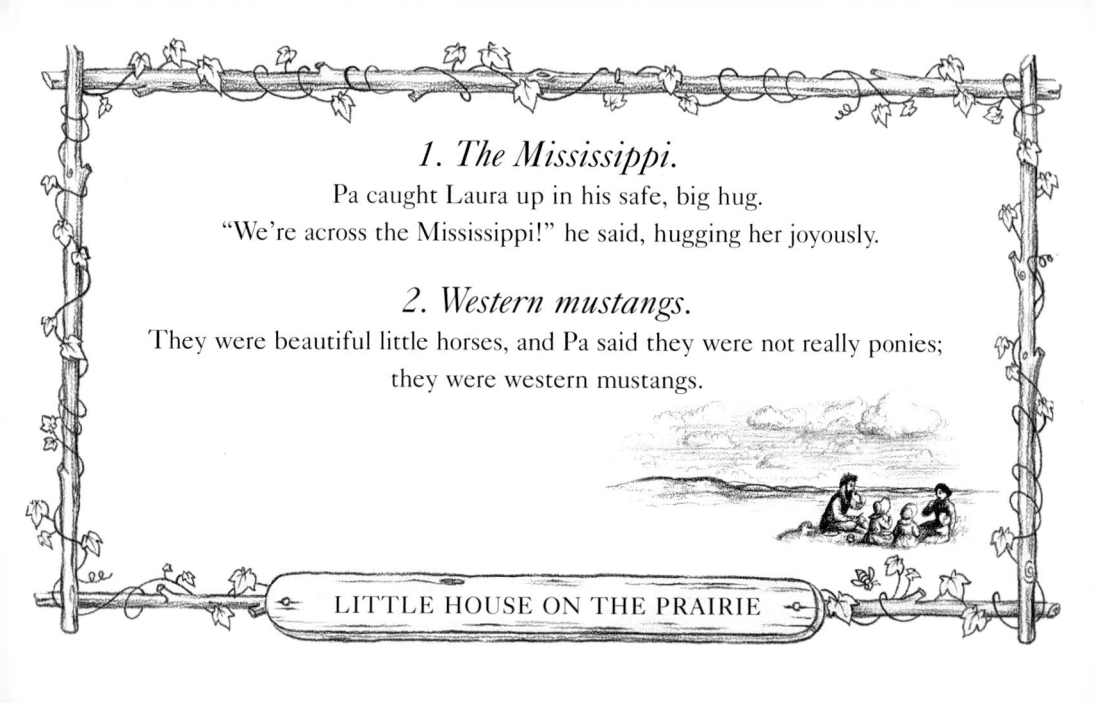

3. What little animals do Laura and Mary try to catch?

4. Why does Laura call Pet's new colt Bunny?

3. Gophers.

Laura and Mary wanted to catch one to take to Ma.

4. Because it looks like a rabbit.

They had never seen a colt with ears so long. Pa said it was a little mule, but Laura said it looked like a jack rabbit. So they named the little colt Bunny.

5. What state does Mr. Edwards tell Laura he is from?

6. What song does Pa play as Mr. Edwards goes home?

5. *Tennessee.*

He bowed to Ma and called her "Ma'am," politely.
But he told Laura that he was a wildcat from Tennessee.

6. *"Old Dan Tucker."*

Far over the prairie rang Pa's big voice and Laura's little one,
and faintly from the creek bottoms came a last whoop from Mr. Edwards.

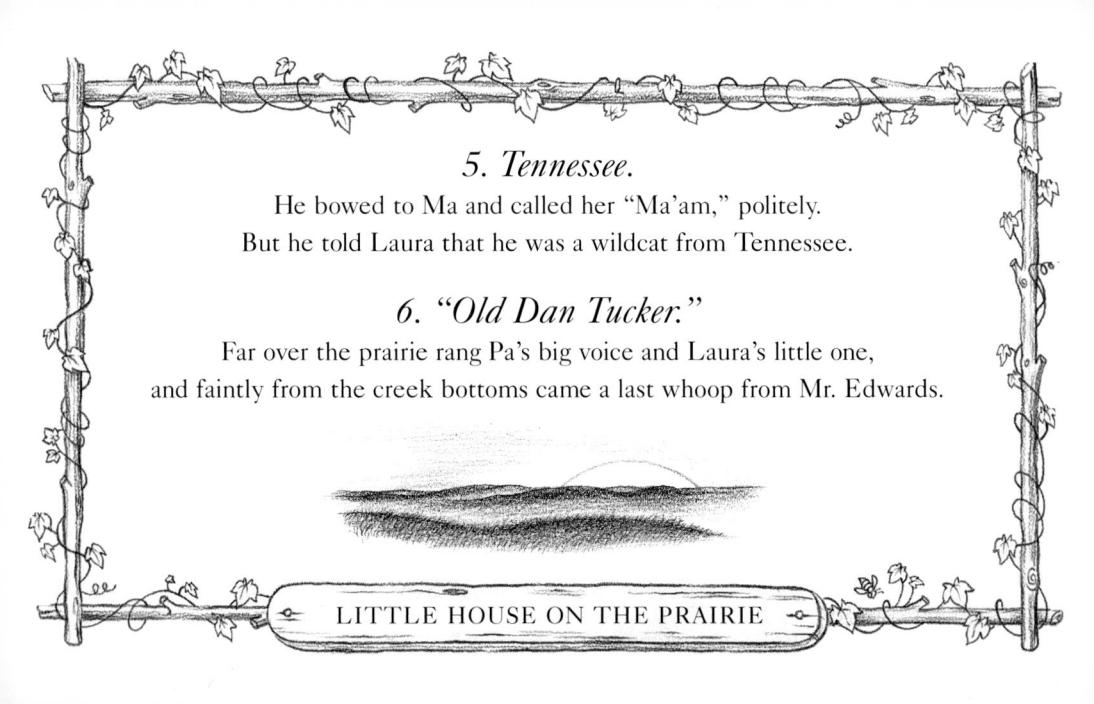

7. What three things do the cowboys give Pa?

8. Where are the cowboys heading with their cattle?

LITTLE HOUSE ON THE PRAIRIE

7. *A cow, a calf, and a hunk of beef.*

The calf was too small to travel, Pa said, and the cow would be too thin to sell, so the cowboys had given them to Pa. They had given him the beef, too.

8. *Fort Dodge, Kansas.*

9. What does Pa make for Ma
when he is getting over the fever 'n' ague?

10. Why won't Ma let Laura and Mary eat watermelon?

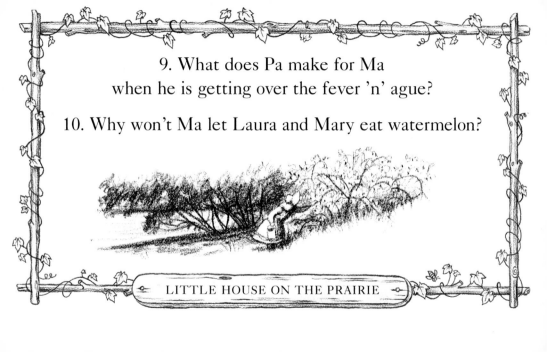

9. A rocking chair.

He wasn't able to work, so he could make a rocking chair for Ma.

10. Because she thinks it causes fever 'n' ague.

Ma would not taste it. She would not let Laura and Mary eat one bite.

LITTLE HOUSE ON THE PRAIRIE

11. What special gift for the house does Pa bring
from Independence?

12. Why do Laura and Mary
think they will have no Christmas?

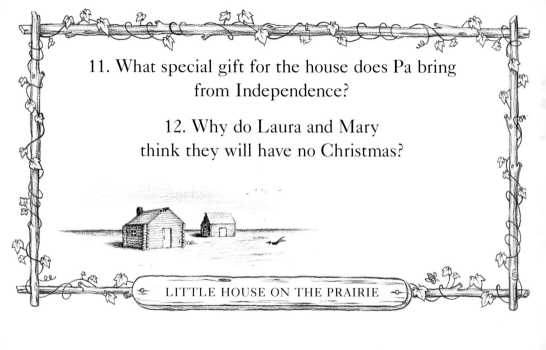

11. Window-glass.

In that square package there were eight small squares of window-glass.
They would have glass windows in their house.

12. Because they think the creek is too high for Santa Claus to cross.

Now they knew they would have no Christmas,
because Santa Claus could not cross that roaring creek.

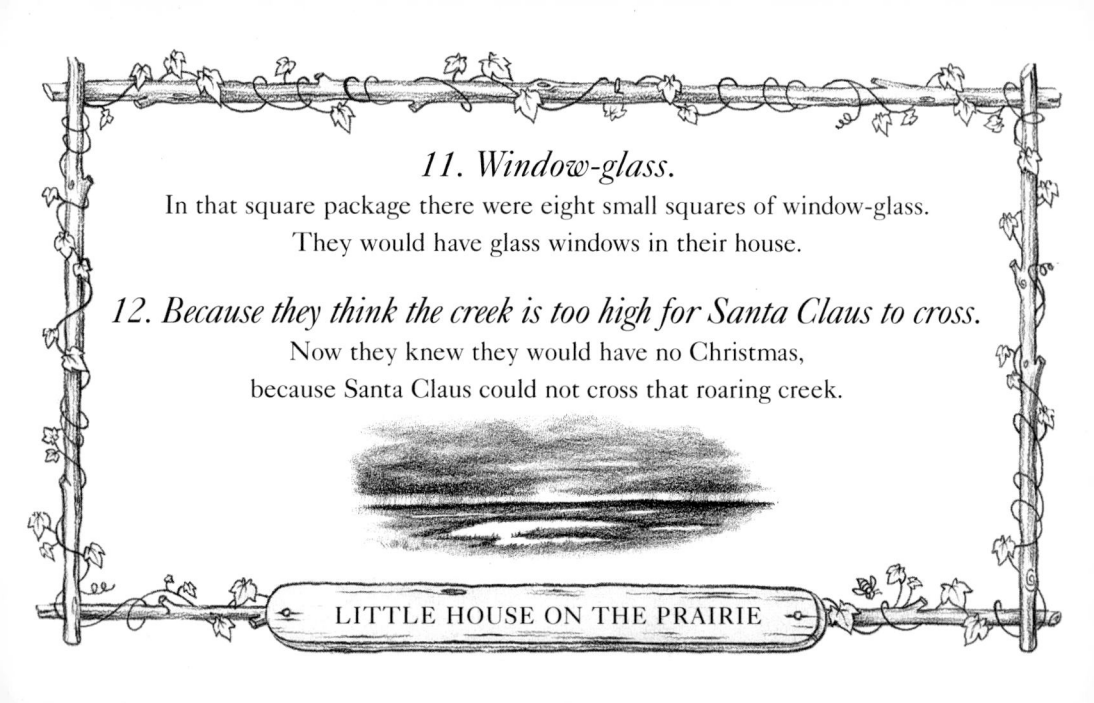

13. Who comes unexpectedly for Christmas?

14. How many sweet potatoes does Mr. Edwards bring?

13. Mr. Edwards.

"Your little ones had to have Christmas," Mr. Edwards replied.

"No creek could stop me, after I fetched them their gifts from Independence."

14. Nine.

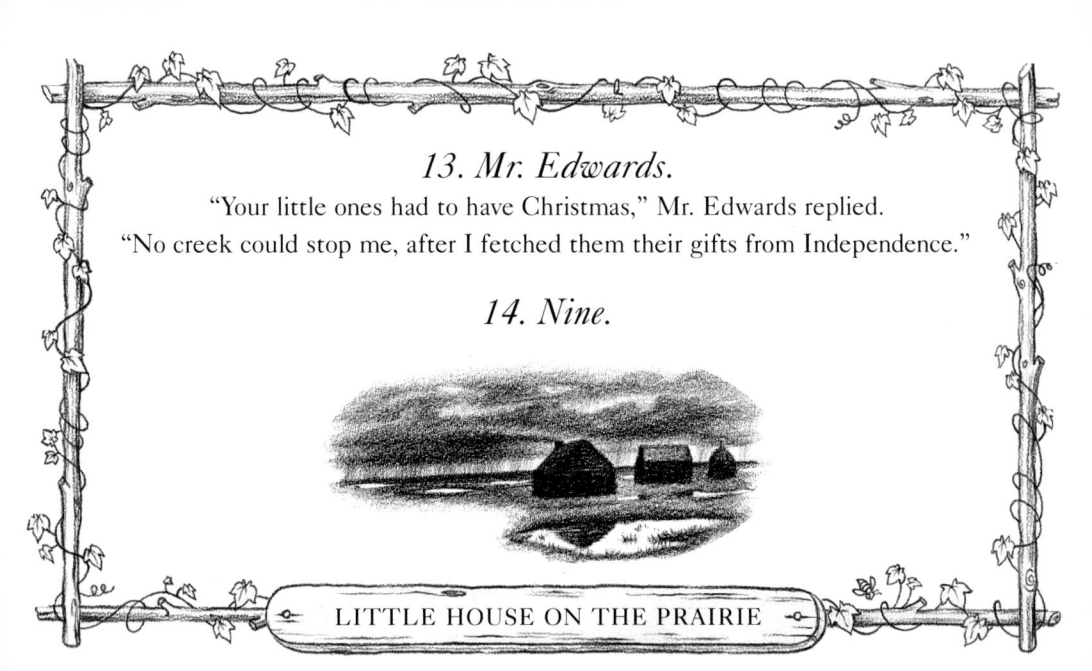

LITTLE HOUSE ON THE PRAIRIE

15. What makes the scream in the night?

16. What presents for Laura and Mary does Pa bring back from town?

15. A panther.

16. Hair combs.
The ribbon in Mary's comb was blue, and the ribbon in Laura's comb was red.

17. What is the name of the Osage Pa talks to
in the woods?

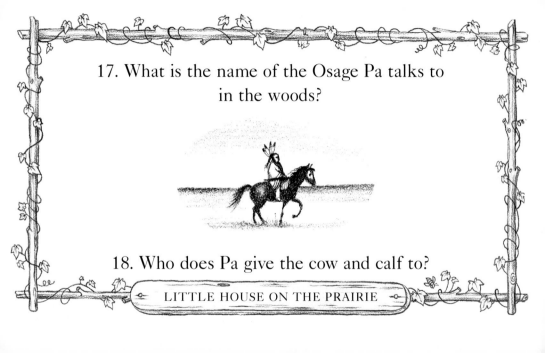

18. Who does Pa give the cow and calf to?

17. *Soldat du Chêne.*

He was an Osage, and they called him a name that meant he was a great soldier.

18. *Mr. Scott.*

Then Pa told Mr. Scott to take the cow and calf.

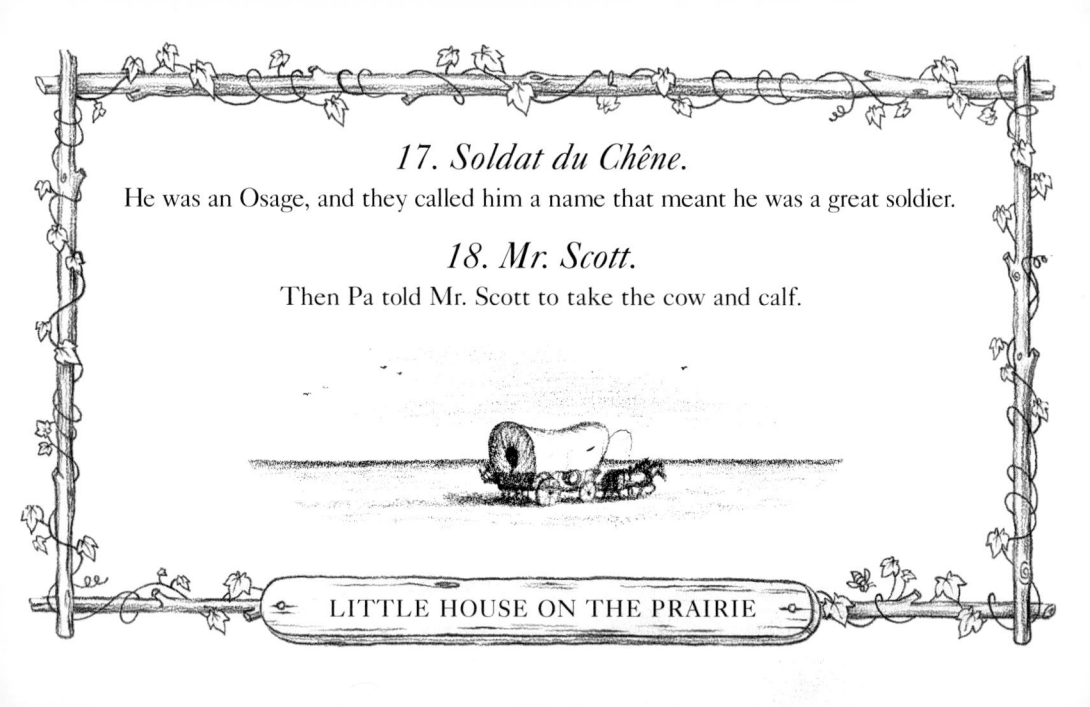

1. In what state does Almanzo live?

2. Who is Mr. Corse?

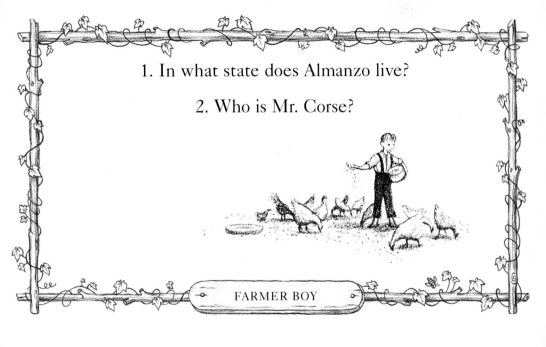

FARMER BOY

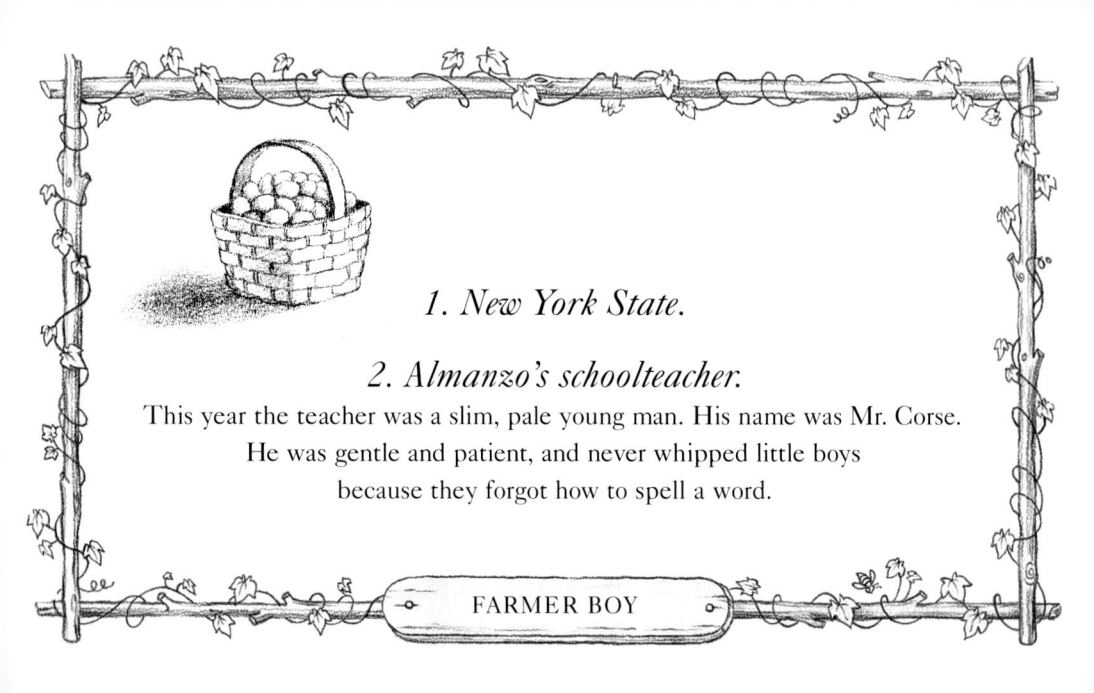

1. New York State.

2. Almanzo's schoolteacher.

This year the teacher was a slim, pale young man. His name was Mr. Corse.
He was gentle and patient, and never whipped little boys
because they forgot how to spell a word.

FARMER BOY

3. What is the name of the town near Almanzo's farm?

4. What does Almanzo pack the ice in to keep it cold?

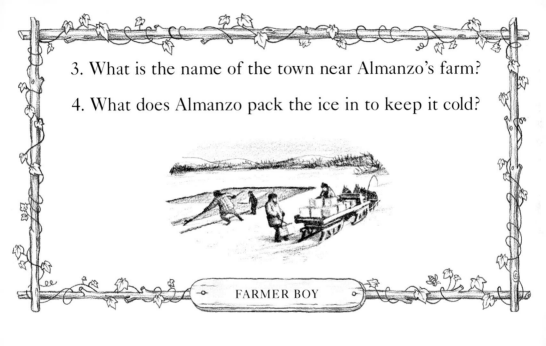

FARMER BOY

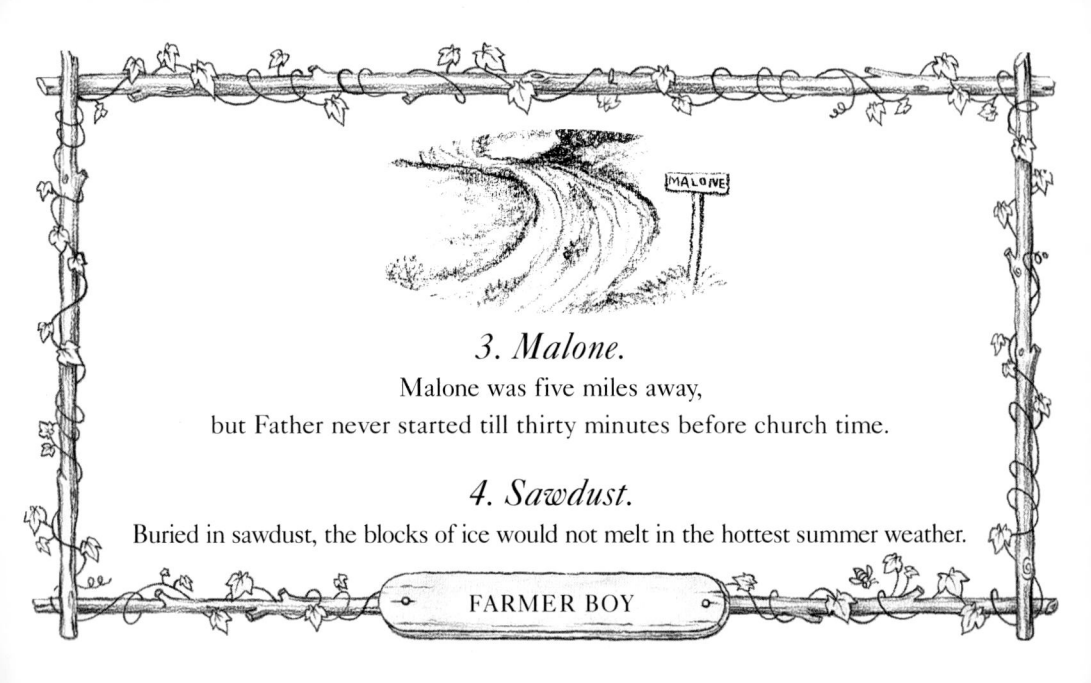

3. Malone.

Malone was five miles away,
but Father never started till thirty minutes before church time.

4. Sawdust.

Buried in sawdust, the blocks of ice would not melt in the hottest summer weather.

FARMER BOY

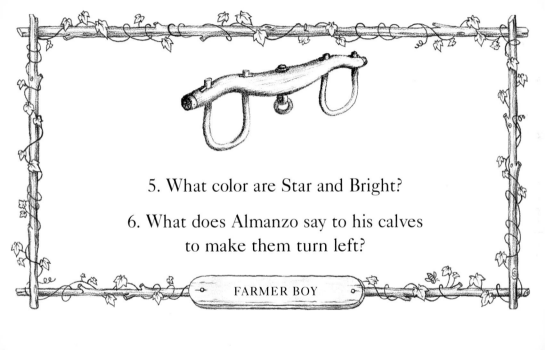

5. What color are Star and Bright?

6. What does Almanzo say to his calves
to make them turn left?

FARMER BOY

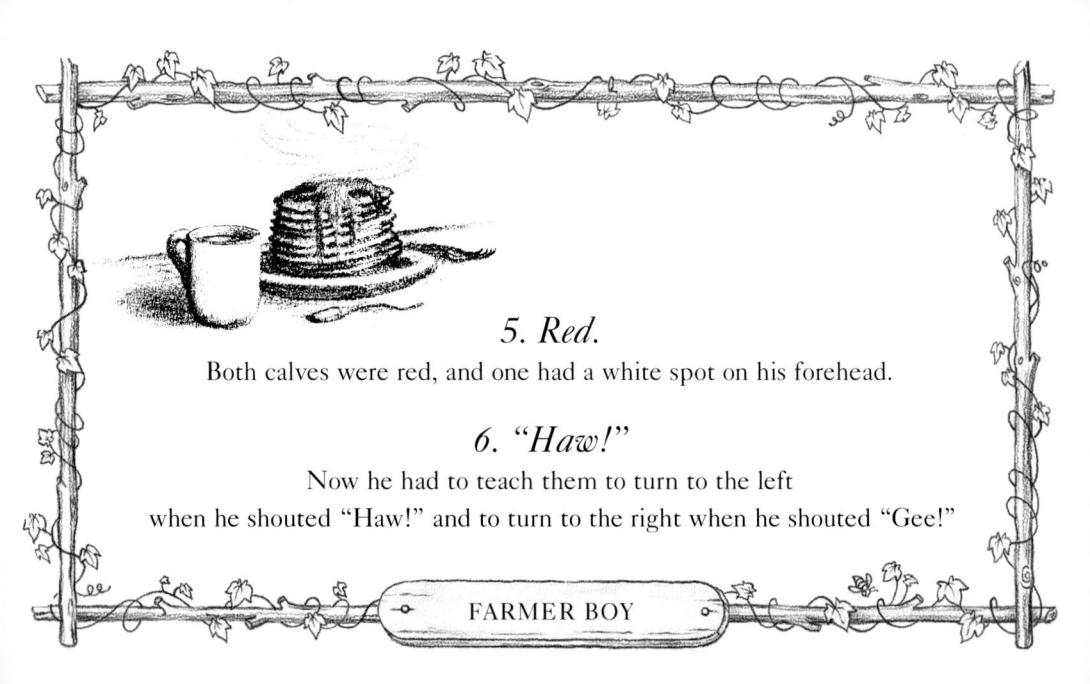

5. *Red.*

Both calves were red, and one had a white spot on his forehead.

6. *"Haw!"*

Now he had to teach them to turn to the left
when he shouted "Haw!" and to turn to the right when he shouted "Gee!"

FARMER BOY

7. What kind of berries does Almanzo dig out of the snow and eat?

8. Who rides in a large, bright-red cart pulled by a white horse?

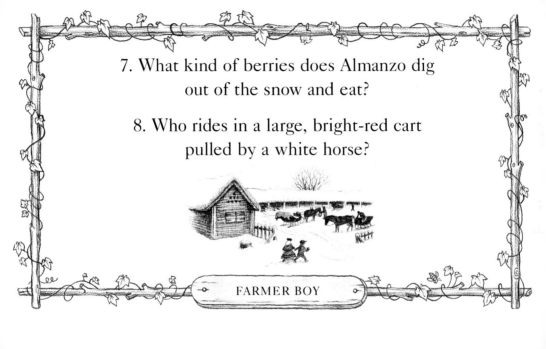

FARMER BOY

7. *Wintergreen berries.*

Nothing else was ever so good as wintergreen berries dug out of the snow.

8. *The tin-peddler.*

His cart was like a little house,
swinging on stout leather straps
between four high wheels.

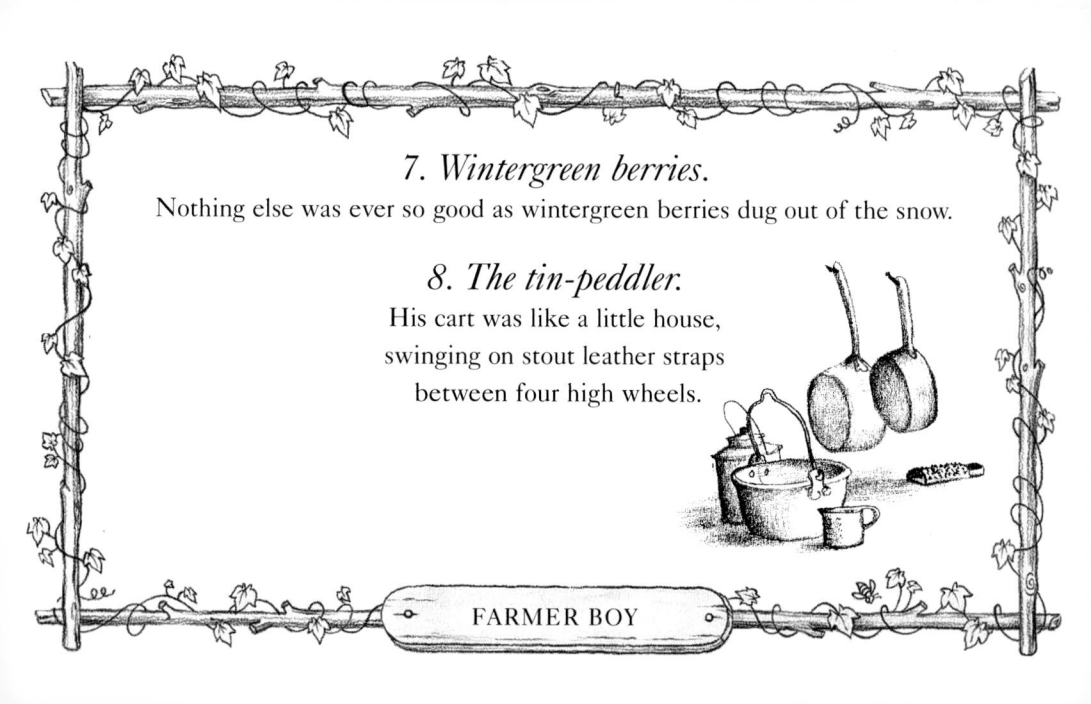

FARMER BOY

9. How does Almanzo "keep up" with Father and Royal during sheep-shearing?

10. What does Almanzo plant in the dark of the moon?

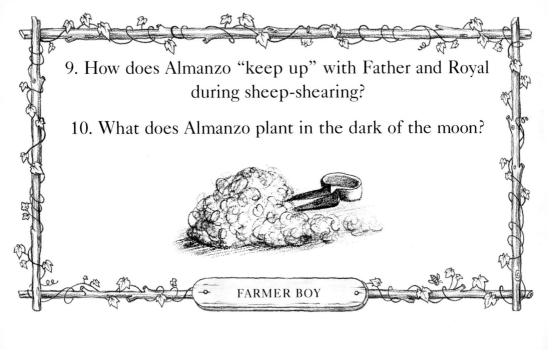

9. He hides an unshorn sheep in the loft.

10. Pumpkin seeds.

He watched the moon anxiously, for in the dark of the moon
in May he could stay out of school and plant pumpkins.

FARMER BOY

11. Who do Mother and Father visit for a week?

12. What does Almanzo throw against the parlor wall?

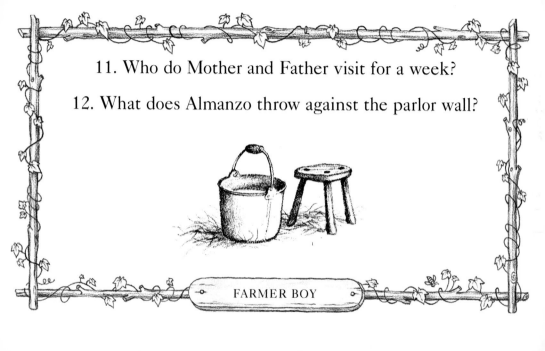

FARMER BOY

11. Uncle Andrew.

One evening at supper Father said, "It's time Mother and I had a vacation. We're thinking of spending a week at Uncle Andrew's."

12. The blacking-brush.

Almanzo didn't mean to throw the blacking-brush. It flew right out of his hand. It sailed past Eliza Jane's head. Smack! it hit the parlor wall.

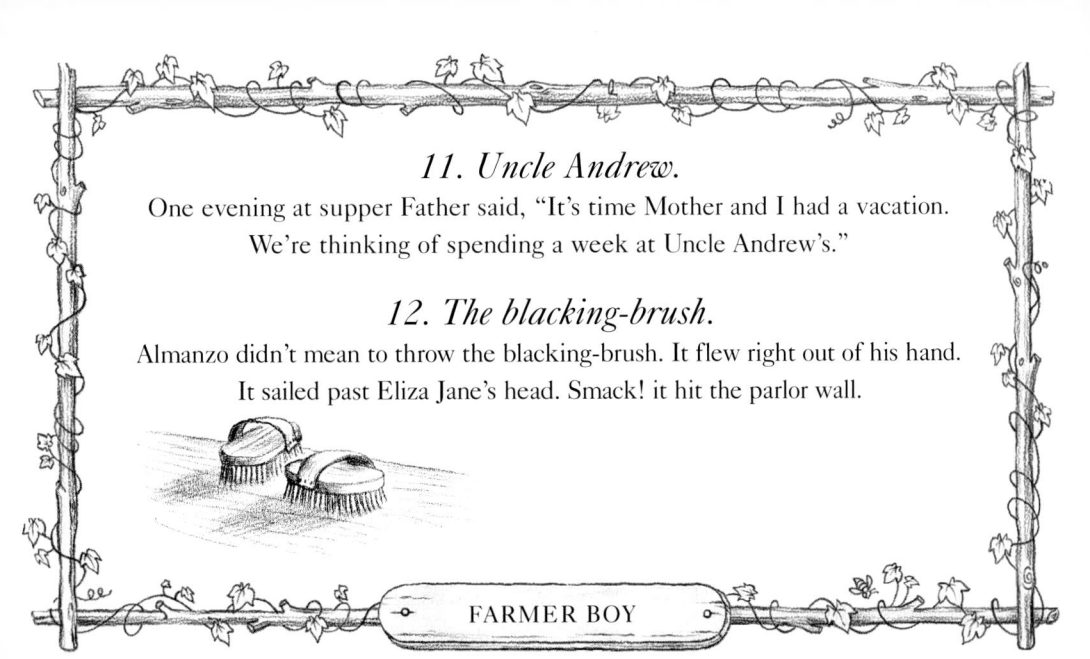

FARMER BOY

13. What does Almanzo win first prize for at the country fair?

14. What kind of shoes does Father think Almanzo is big enough to wear when the cobbler comes?

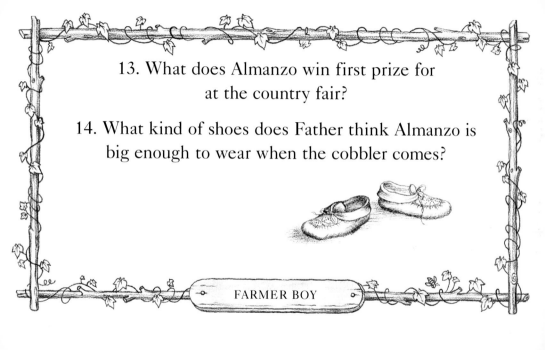

FARMER BOY

13. *A pumpkin.*

He held out the blue ribbon, above another pumpkin.
He leaned, and stretched out his arm slowly,
and he thrust the pin into Almanzo's pumpkin.

14. *Boots.*

Almanzo could hardly believe it.
He had wanted boots for so long.

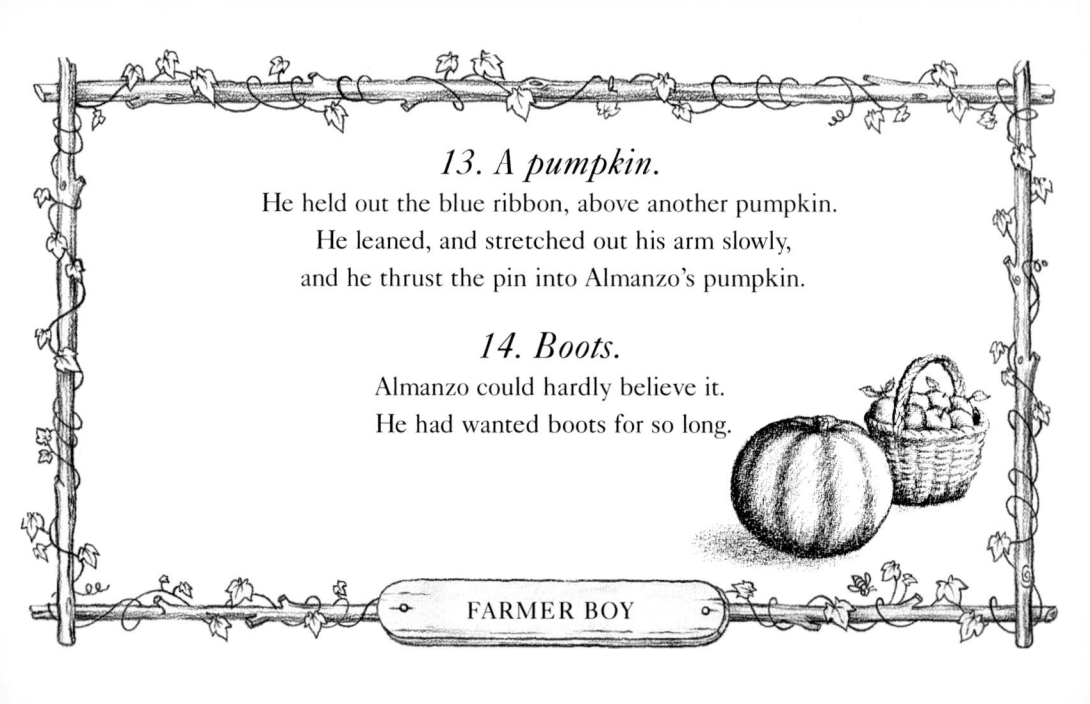

15. How much money is in Mr. Thompson's wallet?

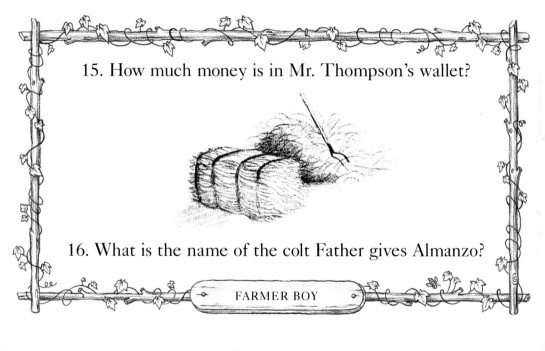

16. What is the name of the colt Father gives Almanzo?

FARMER BOY

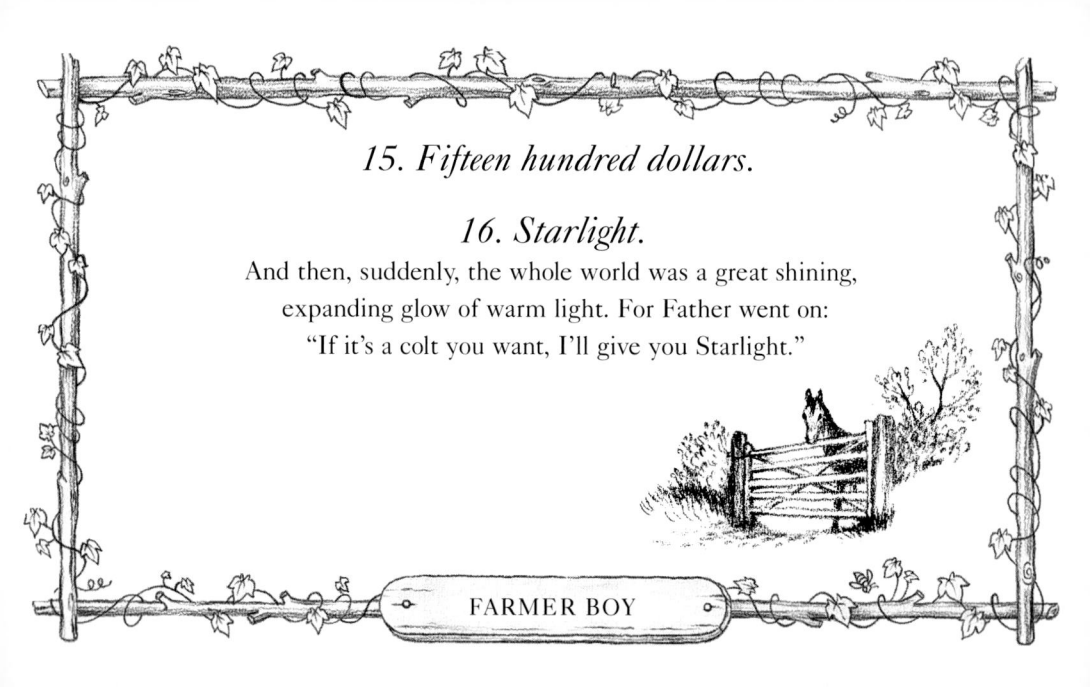

15. *Fifteen hundred dollars.*

16. *Starlight.*

And then, suddenly, the whole world was a great shining,
expanding glow of warm light. For Father went on:
"If it's a colt you want, I'll give you Starlight."

FARMER BOY

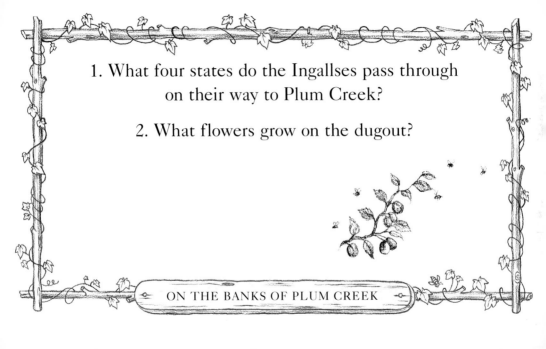

1. What four states do the Ingallses pass through
   on their way to Plum Creek?

2. What flowers grow on the dugout?

ON THE BANKS OF PLUM CREEK

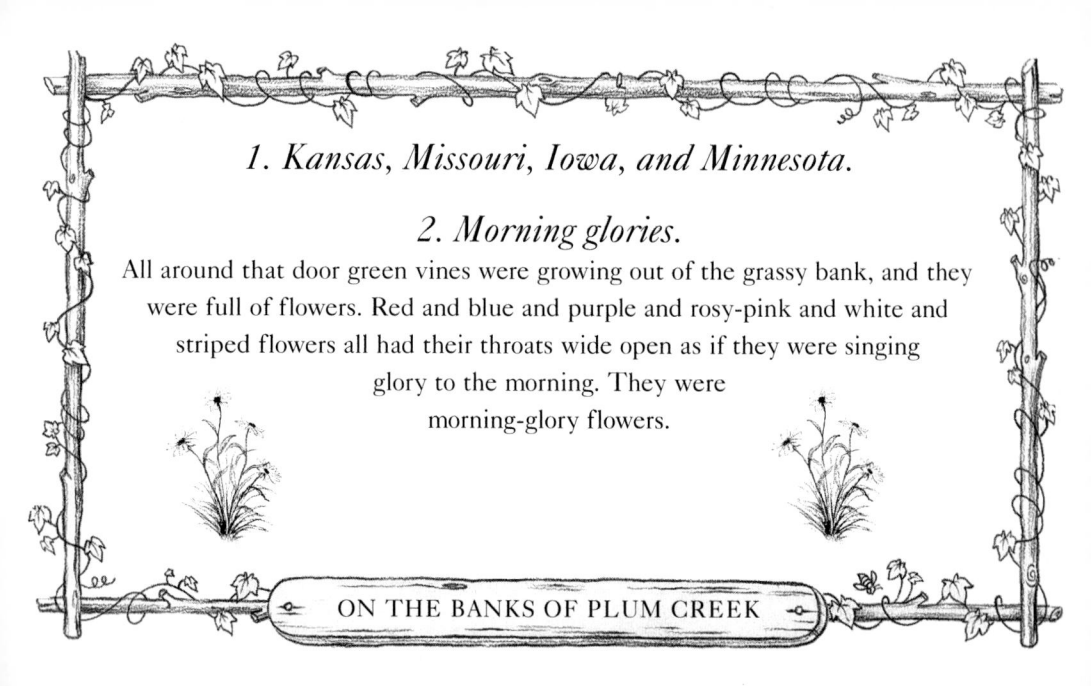

1. Kansas, Missouri, Iowa, and Minnesota.

2. Morning glories.

All around that door green vines were growing out of the grassy bank, and they were full of flowers. Red and blue and purple and rosy-pink and white and striped flowers all had their throats wide open as if they were singing glory to the morning. They were morning-glory flowers.

ON THE BANKS OF PLUM CREEK

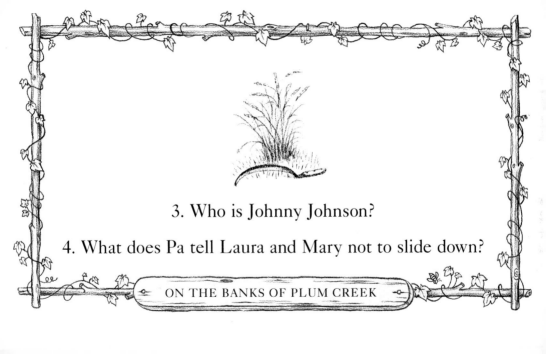

3. Who is Johnny Johnson?

4. What does Pa tell Laura and Mary not to slide down?

ON THE BANKS OF PLUM CREEK

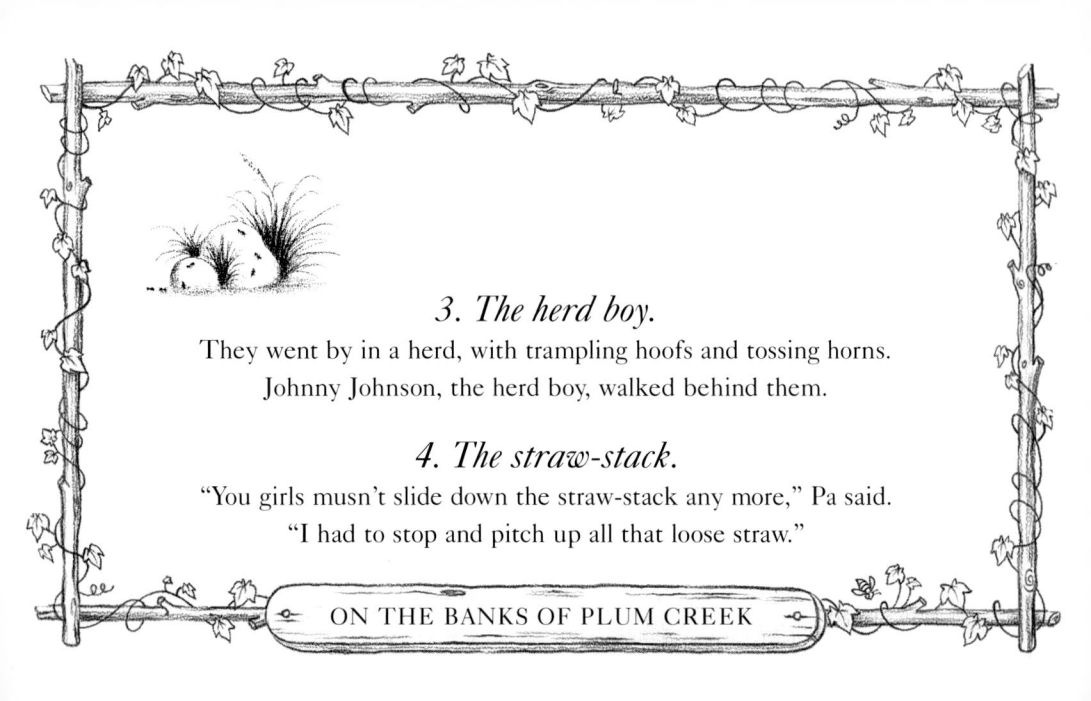

3. The herd boy.

They went by in a herd, with trampling hoofs and tossing horns.
Johnny Johnson, the herd boy, walked behind them.

4. The straw-stack.

"You girls musn't slide down the straw-stack any more," Pa said.
"I had to stop and pitch up all that loose straw."

ON THE BANKS OF PLUM CREEK

5. What is the "wonderful house" made of?

6. What surprise for Ma does Pa hide in the lean-to?

ON THE BANKS OF PLUM CREEK

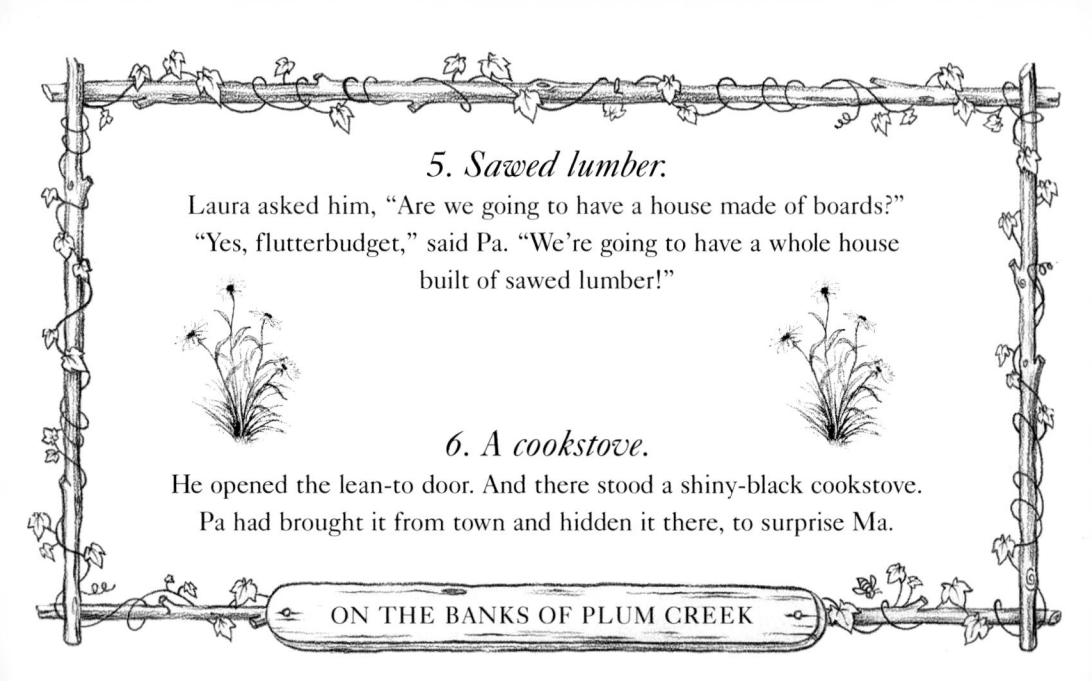

5. *Sawed lumber.*

Laura asked him, "Are we going to have a house made of boards?"

"Yes, flutterbudget," said Pa. "We're going to have a whole house built of sawed lumber!"

6. *A cookstove.*

He opened the lean-to door. And there stood a shiny-black cookstove. Pa had brought it from town and hidden it there, to surprise Ma.

ON THE BANKS OF PLUM CREEK

7. What does Sandy Kennedy call Laura and Mary
the first day of school?

8. How much does the slate pencil cost?

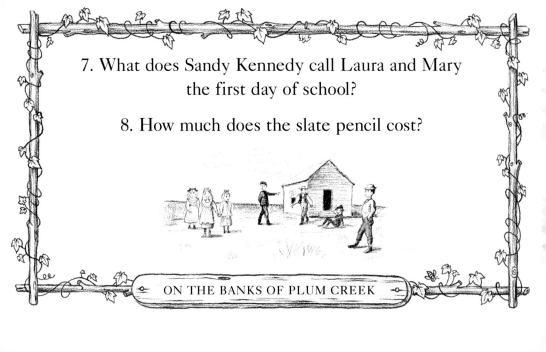

ON THE BANKS OF PLUM CREEK

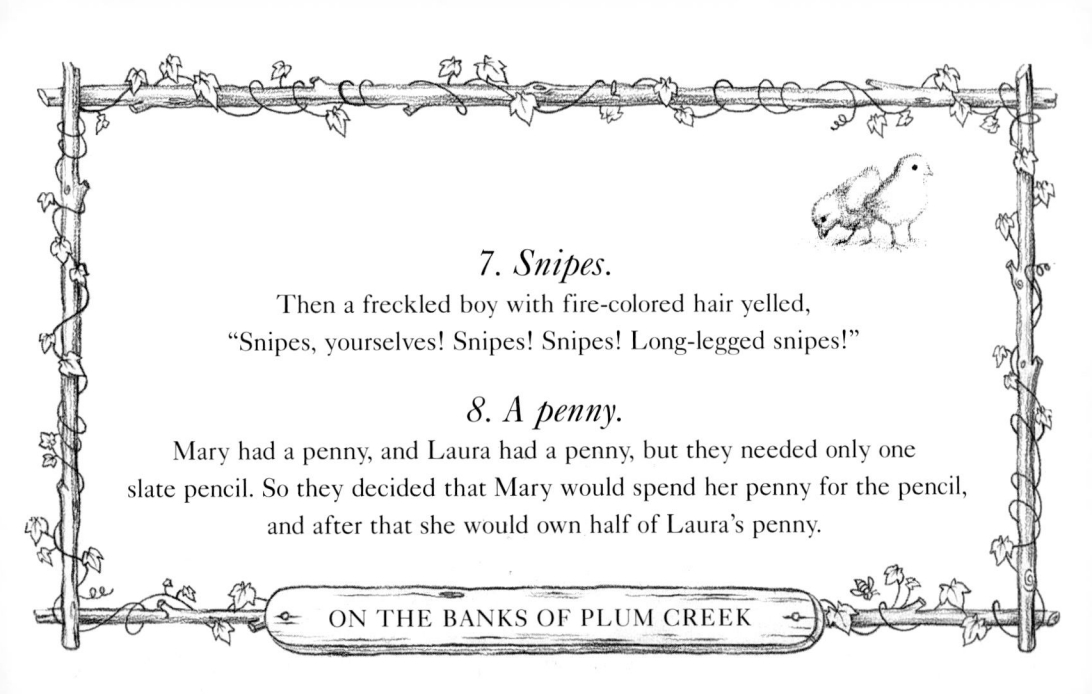

7. *Snipes.*

Then a freckled boy with fire-colored hair yelled,
"Snipes, yourselves! Snipes! Snipes! Long-legged snipes!"

8. *A penny.*

Mary had a penny, and Laura had a penny, but they needed only one
slate pencil. So they decided that Mary would spend her penny for the pencil,
and after that she would own half of Laura's penny.

ON THE BANKS OF PLUM CREEK

9. What game does Nellie always want to play at recess?

10. Where does Laura read *Mother Goose*?

ON THE BANKS OF PLUM CREEK

9. Ring-around-a-rosy.

The little girls always played ring-around-a-rosy,
because Nellie Oleson said to.

10. At Nellie's party.

Laura had not known there were
such wonderful books in the world.

11. What kind of cakes does Ma serve
    at Laura and Mary's party?

12. What is the glittering cloud?

11. *Vanity cakes.*

"Vanity cakes," said Ma. "Because they are all puffed up,
like vanity, with nothing solid inside."

12. *Grasshoppers.*

The cloud was hailing grasshoppers. The cloud *was* grasshoppers.

13. What does Pa ask Ma to take good care of while he is working in the east?

14. What piece of clothing is Laura's favorite Christmas gift?

13. *His fiddle.*

"Take good care of the old fiddle, Caroline," he said. "It puts heart into a man."

14. *A fur cape and muff.*

"For me?" Laura said. "For me?" Then everything else vanished while with both arms she hugged the soft furs to her.

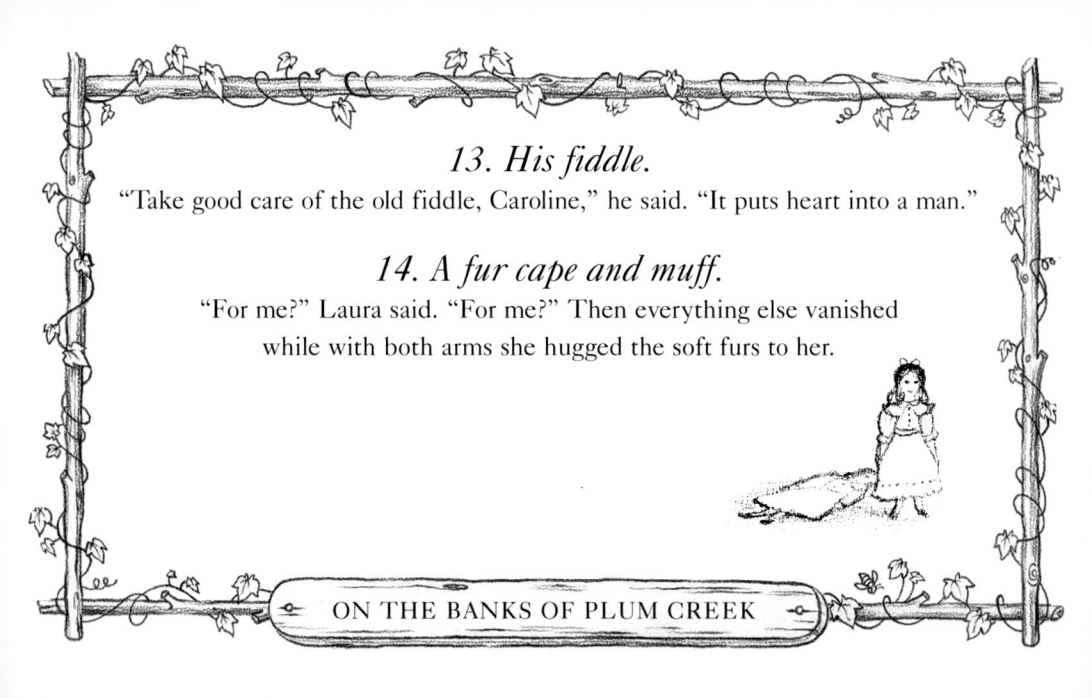

ON THE BANKS OF PLUM CREEK

15. What do Laura and Carrie use to make pictures on the windows?

16. How many days is Pa caught in the blizzard?

15. Thimbles.

Ma gave her thimble to Laura, and Mary's thimble to Carrie,
and she showed them that pressing the thimbles into the frost
on the windows made perfect circles.

16. Four days.

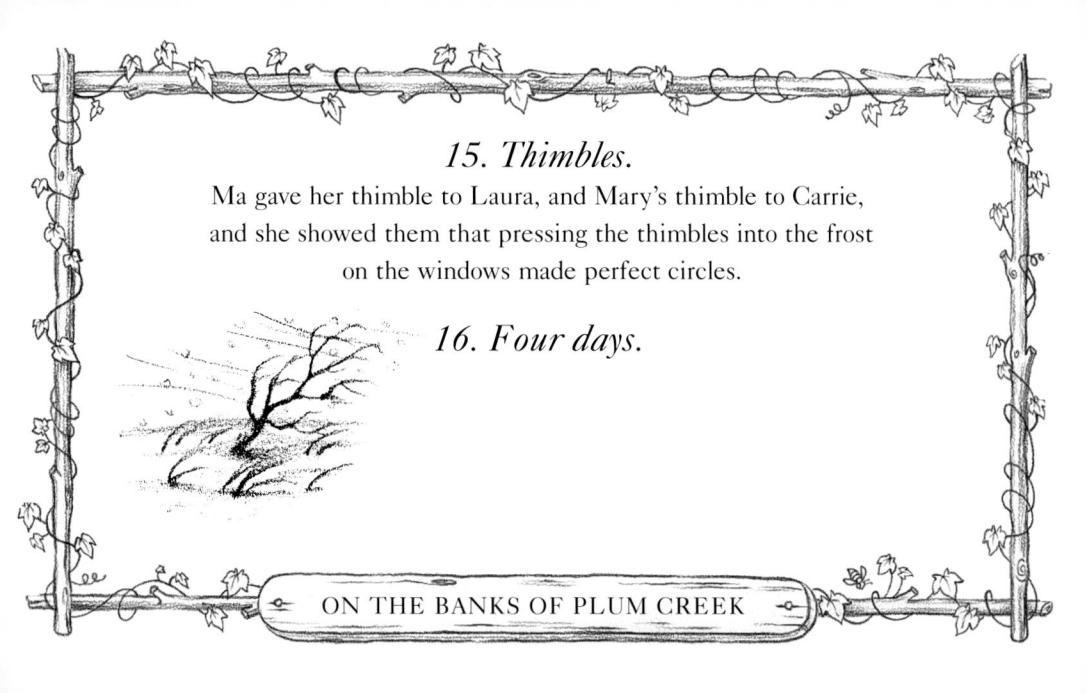

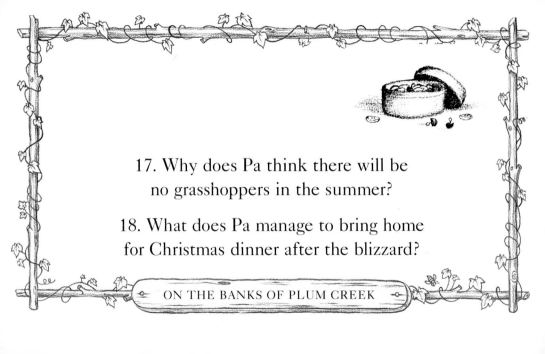

17. Why does Pa think there will be
no grasshoppers in the summer?

18. What does Pa manage to bring home
for Christmas dinner after the blizzard?

ON THE BANKS OF PLUM CREEK

17. Because the winter was so cold.

"We won't have any grasshoppers next summer.
They say in town that grasshoppers come only when the summers
are hot and dry and the winters are mild."

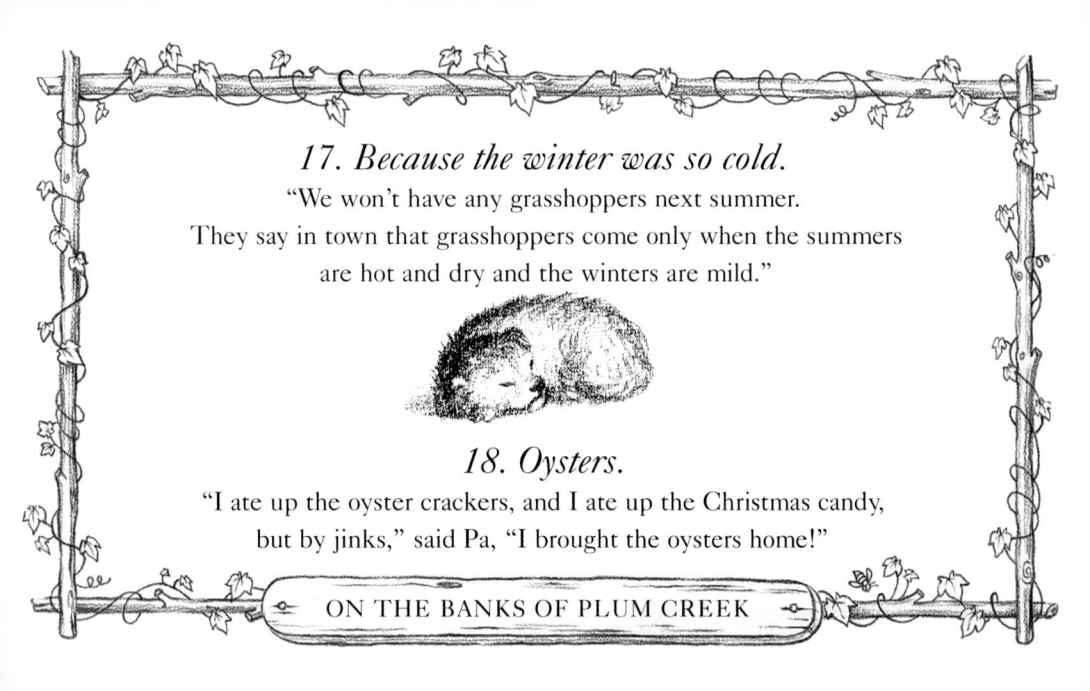

18. Oysters.

"I ate up the oyster crackers, and I ate up the Christmas candy,
but by jinks," said Pa, "I brought the oysters home!"

ON THE BANKS OF PLUM CREEK

1. Which relative comes to visit the Ingallses unexpectedly while they are living at Plum Creek?

2. How far can the train that Ma and the girls take to Tracy go in one hour?

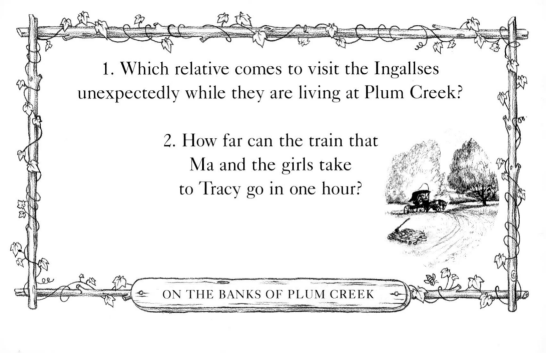

1. Aunt Docia.

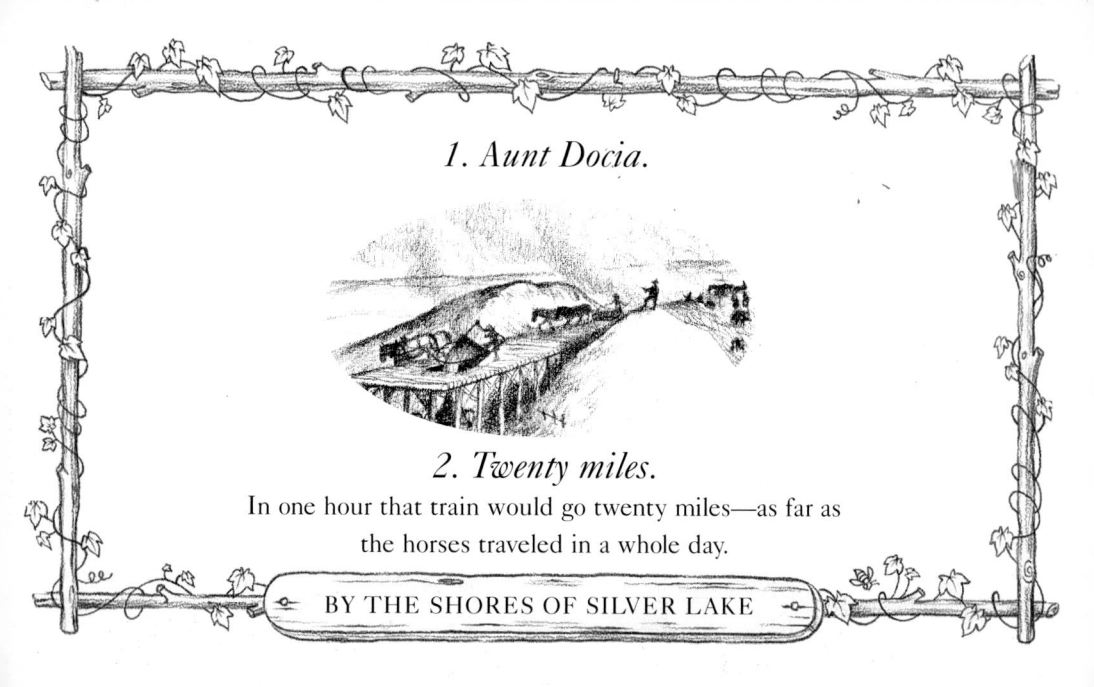

2. Twenty miles.

In one hour that train would go twenty miles—as far as
the horses traveled in a whole day.

3. What do Laura and Lena pick up from the homesteader's wife?

4. What does Lena teach Laura to do in the afternoon?

3. The washing.

A homesteader's wife did Aunt Docia's washing; she lived three miles away
so they'd have a six-mile drive.

4. Ride a horse.

Lena held her pony by the forelock with one hand, and bending down
she held her other hand for Laura to step onto.

BY THE SHORES OF SILVER LAKE

5. What bird does Pa shoot by mistake?

6. Whose house do the Ingallses live in for the winter?

BY THE SHORES OF SILVER LAKE

5. A swan.

One day Pa came home from hunting, bringing a great, snow-white bird.

6. The surveyors' house.

Laura thought that there must have been a great many surveyors to need so much space. This would be by far the largest house she had ever lived in.

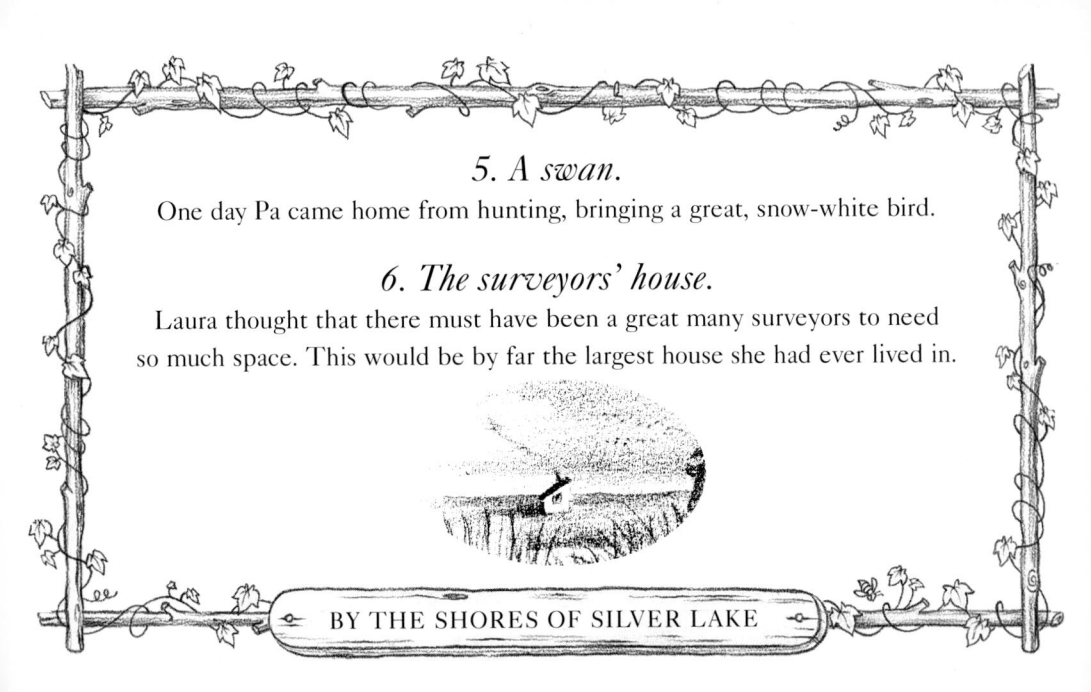

7. What is the "prairie cure" supposed to cure?

8. What two dances does Pa teach Laura and Carrie?

7. *Consumption.*

"Yes, I know, Caroline. It's true enough, I guess, these prairies
are about the only thing that cures consumption."

8. *The polka and the waltz.*

Laura and Carrie waltzed across the room and back,
and around and around the room.

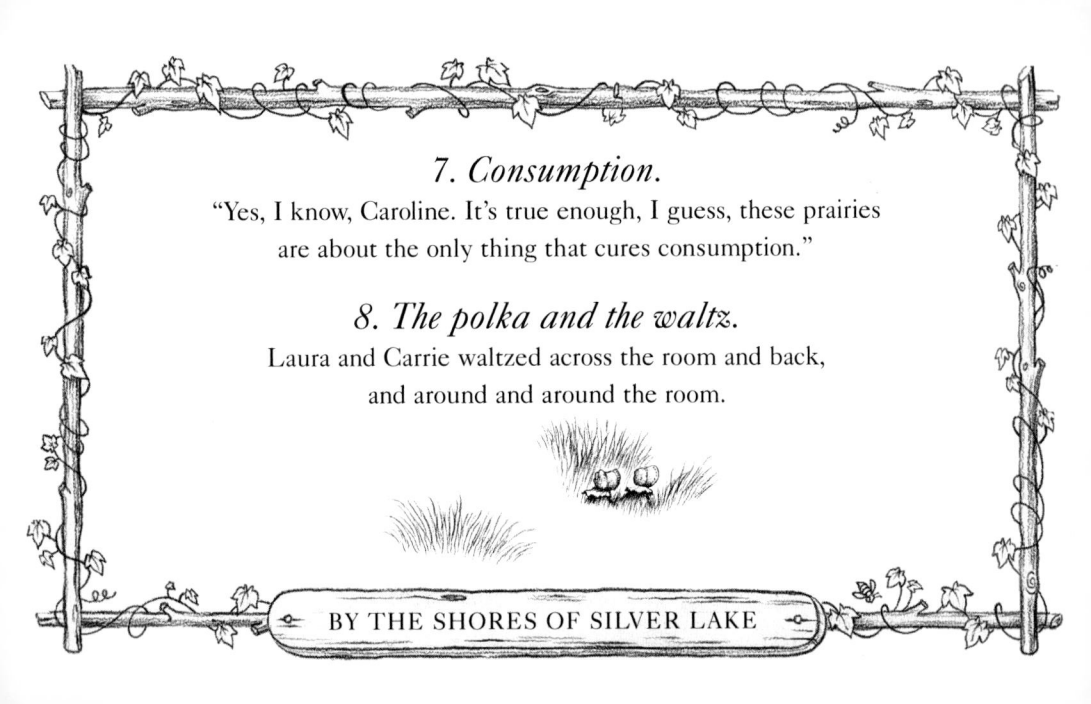

BY THE SHORES OF SILVER LAKE

9. Why do Laura and Carrie run back to the house after they have been sliding in the moonlight?

10. With what is Grace's Christmas coat trimmed?

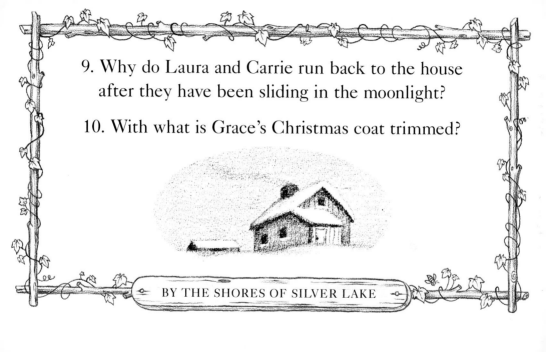

BY THE SHORES OF SILVER LAKE

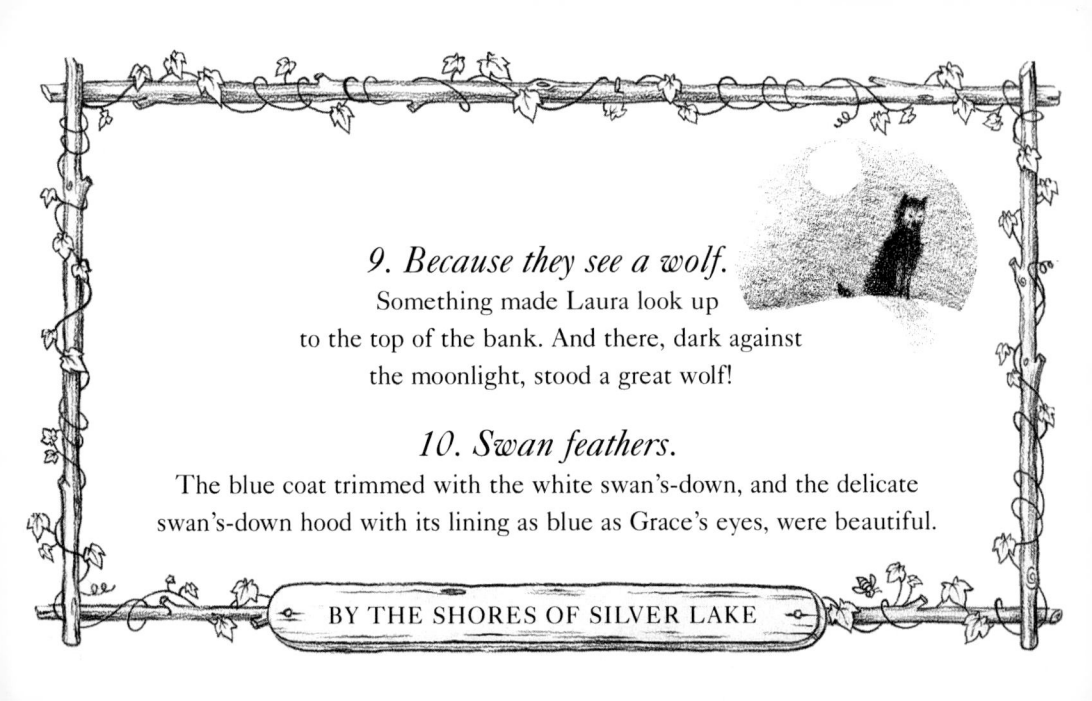

9. *Because they see a wolf.*

Something made Laura look up
to the top of the bank. And there, dark against
the moonlight, stood a great wolf!

10. *Swan feathers.*

The blue coat trimmed with the white swan's-down, and the delicate
swan's-down hood with its lining as blue as Grace's eyes, were beautiful.

BY THE SHORES OF SILVER LAKE

11. Whose laugh is contagious?

12. What surprise does Mrs. Boast "smuggle" into the Ingallses' house on Christmas Eve?

11. *Mr. Boast's.*

Mr. Boast laughed, and in the house everyone laughed, even Ma. . . .
Mrs. Boast was laughing too. "It's contagious," she said.

12. *Popcorn.*

They smuggled the bag into the house and hid it in the pantry,
whispering to tell Ma what it was.

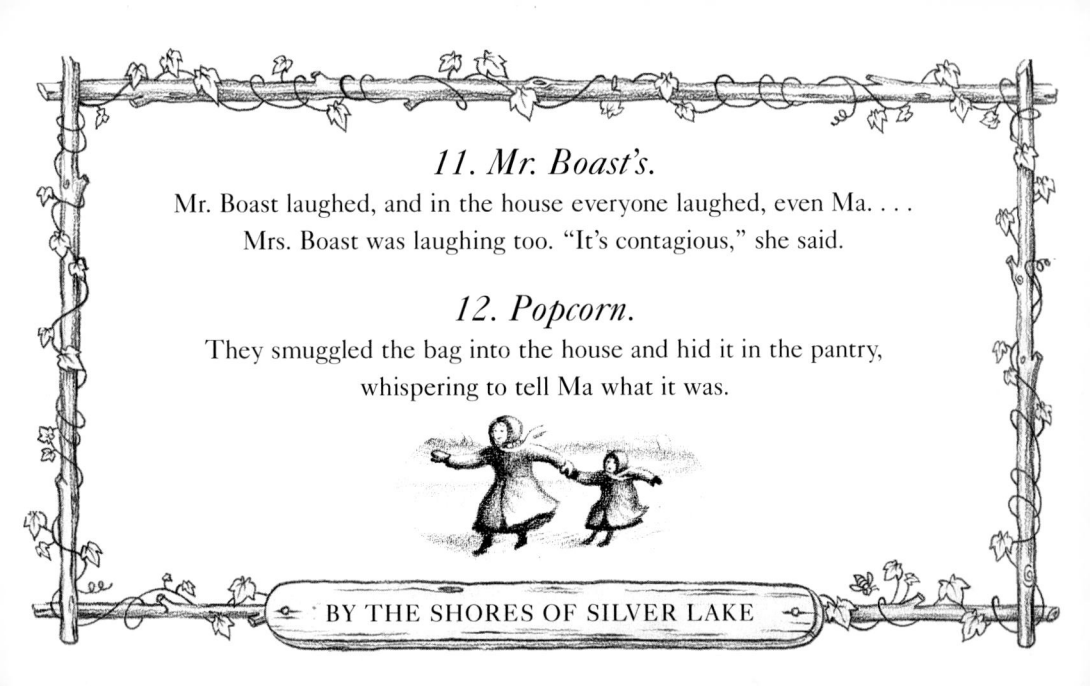

13. Who tells Mary that there is a school for the blind?

14. Who helps Pa file his homestead claim?

13. Reverend Alden.

"Laura," Mary whispered, "Reverend Alden told me there are colleges for blind people."

14. Mr. Edwards.

"Right then, quick as a wink, somebody landed like a ton of bricks on the Huron man. 'Go in, Ingalls!' he yelled. 'I'll fix 'im! Yow-ee-ee!' "

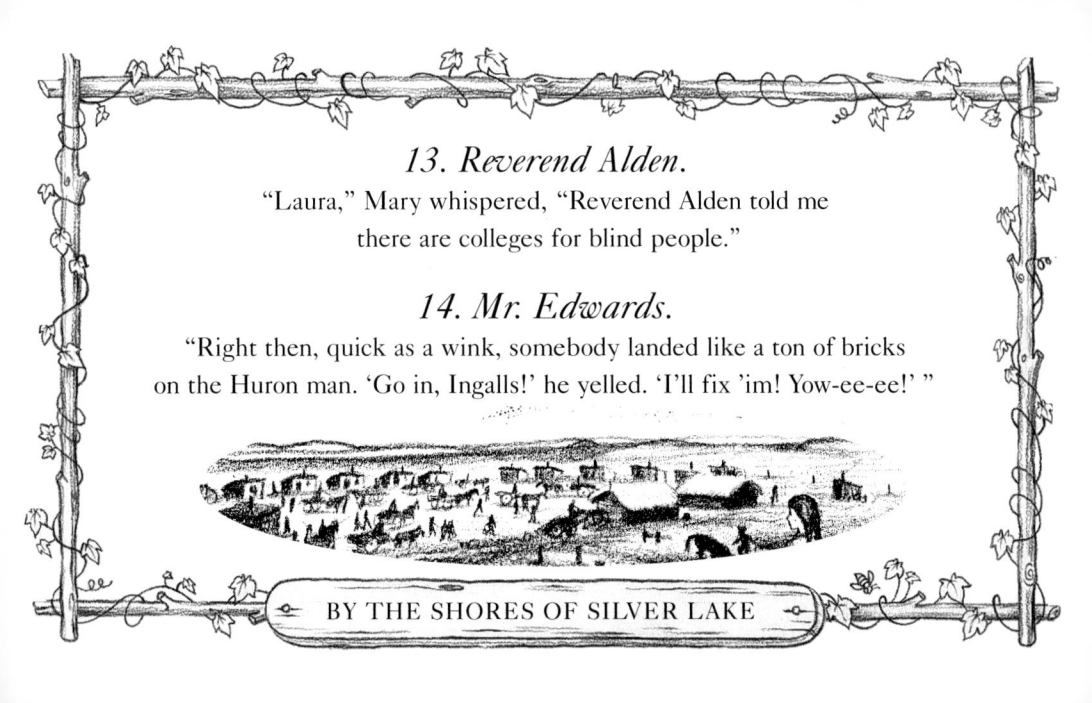

BY THE SHORES OF SILVER LAKE

15. Who gets lost while Pa is planting trees?

16. What flowers grow in the buffalo wallow?

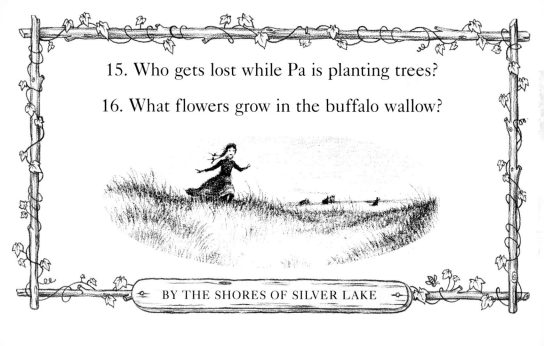

BY THE SHORES OF SILVER LAKE

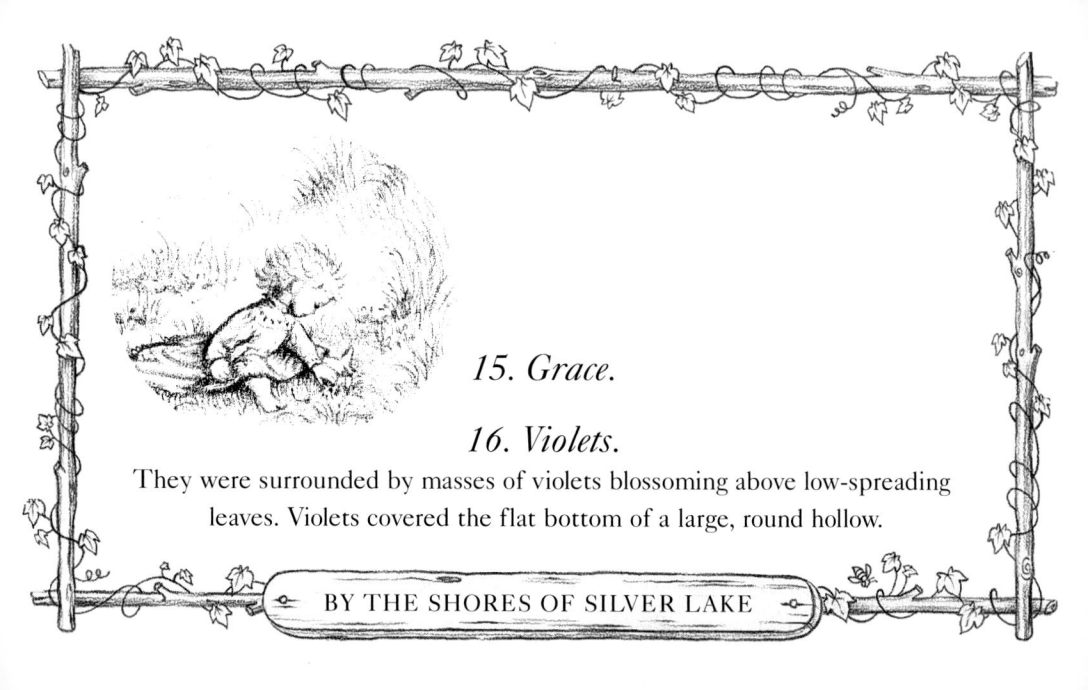

15. *Grace.*

16. *Violets.*

They were surrounded by masses of violets blossoming above low-spreading leaves. Violets covered the flat bottom of a large, round hollow.

BY THE SHORES OF SILVER LAKE

1. What does Laura help Pa make at the beginning of the book?

2. What is the muskrat house made of?

THE LONG WINTER

1. Hay.

"Pa," Laura said, "Why can't I help you make hay? Please let me, Pa. Please."

2. Grass and mud.

The muskrats had gnawed
dry grass to bits and mixed the bits
well with mud to make a good
plaster for their house.

3. What does Pa ask Laura to buy in town for him?

4. Who do Laura and Carrie meet on their way back from town?

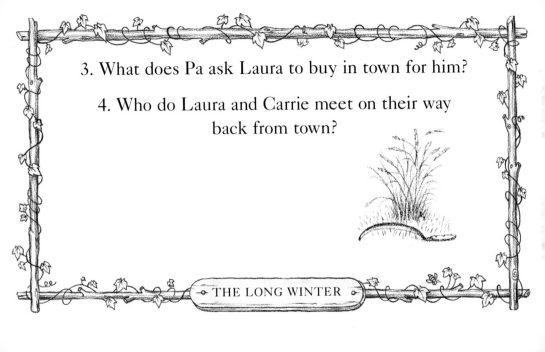

3. A mowing-machine section.

Laura said, "Pa wants a mowing-machine section, please." The man on the plow said, "He's broke one, has he?" and Laura said, "Yes, sir."

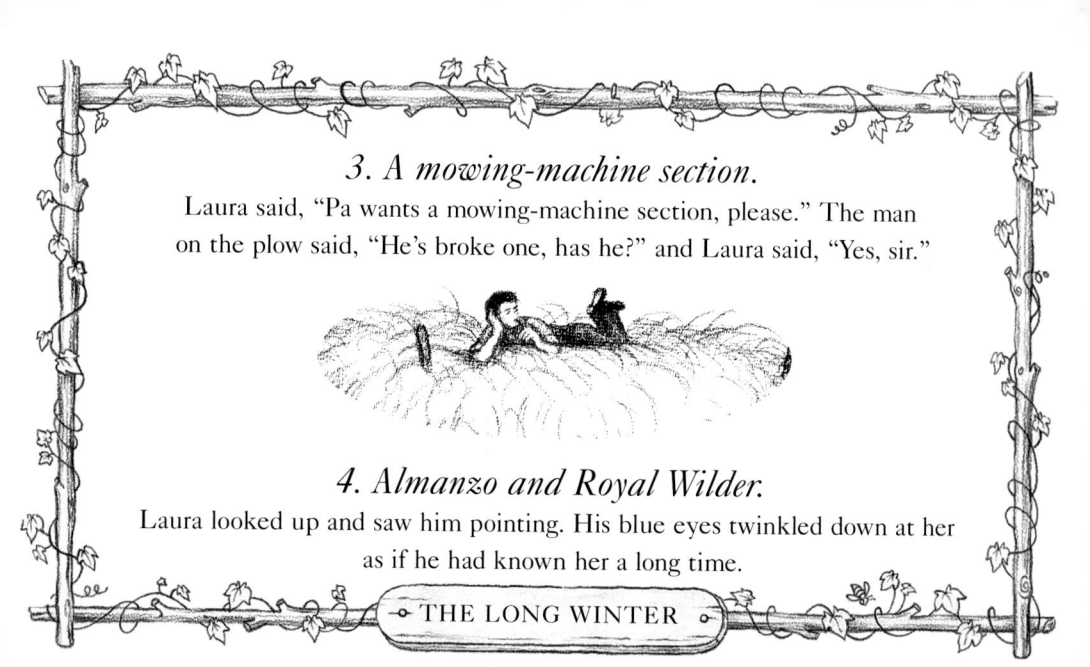

4. Almanzo and Royal Wilder.

Laura looked up and saw him pointing. His blue eyes twinkled down at her as if he had known her a long time.

THE LONG WINTER

5. What kind of pie does Ma bake as a surprise for Pa?

6. What is cambric tea?

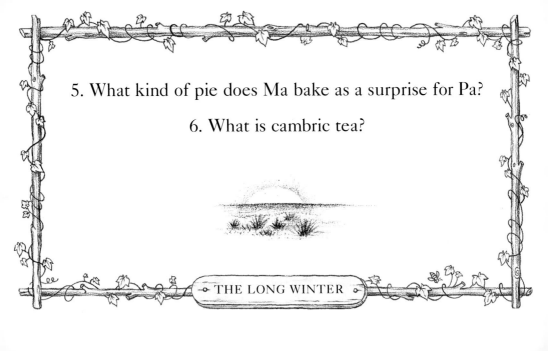

5. *Green pumpkin pie.*

"Hurry and get the work done," said Ma. "And then, Laura, you go to the corn-patch and bring me a green pumpkin. I'm going to make a pie!"

6. *Weak tea and milk.*

Cambric tea was hot water and milk, with only a taste of tea in it, but little girls felt grown-up when their mothers let them drink cambric tea.

THE LONG WINTER

7. In what month does the first blizzard come?

8. What does Laura call the bird that Pa finds after the first blizzard?

7. *October.*

"A b-b-b-b-blizzard!" Ma chattered. "In Oc-October. I n-n-never heard of . . ."

8. *A great auk.*

"It's a great auk," Laura declared. "Only it's a little one."

9. What is the name of the street that Pa's store building is on?

10. What building does Laura bump into during the second blizzard?

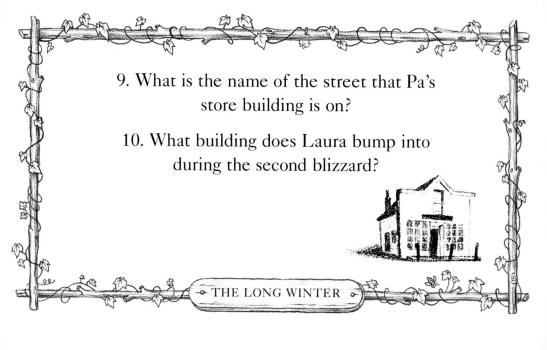

9. Main Street.
Pa's store building was one of the best in town.
It stood by itself on the east side of Main Street.

10. Mead's Hotel.
They followed along the side of that building till they came to the front of it,
and it was Mead's Hotel, at the very north end of Main Street.

⊸ THE LONG WINTER ⊶

1. What gift does Mr. Edwards leave for Mary?

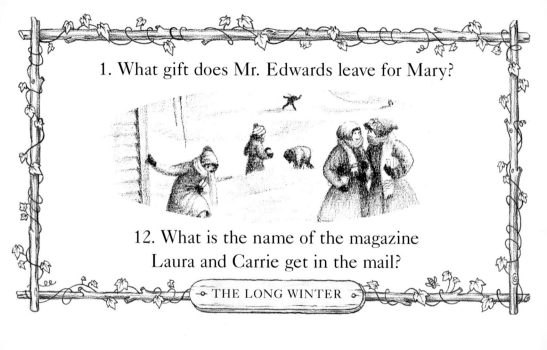

12. What is the name of the magazine
Laura and Carrie get in the mail?

THE LONG WINTER

11. A *twenty dollar bill.*

Laura cried, "Mary! A twenty dollar—You dropped a twenty dollar bill!"

"I couldn't!" Mary exclaimed.

"That Edwards," said Pa.

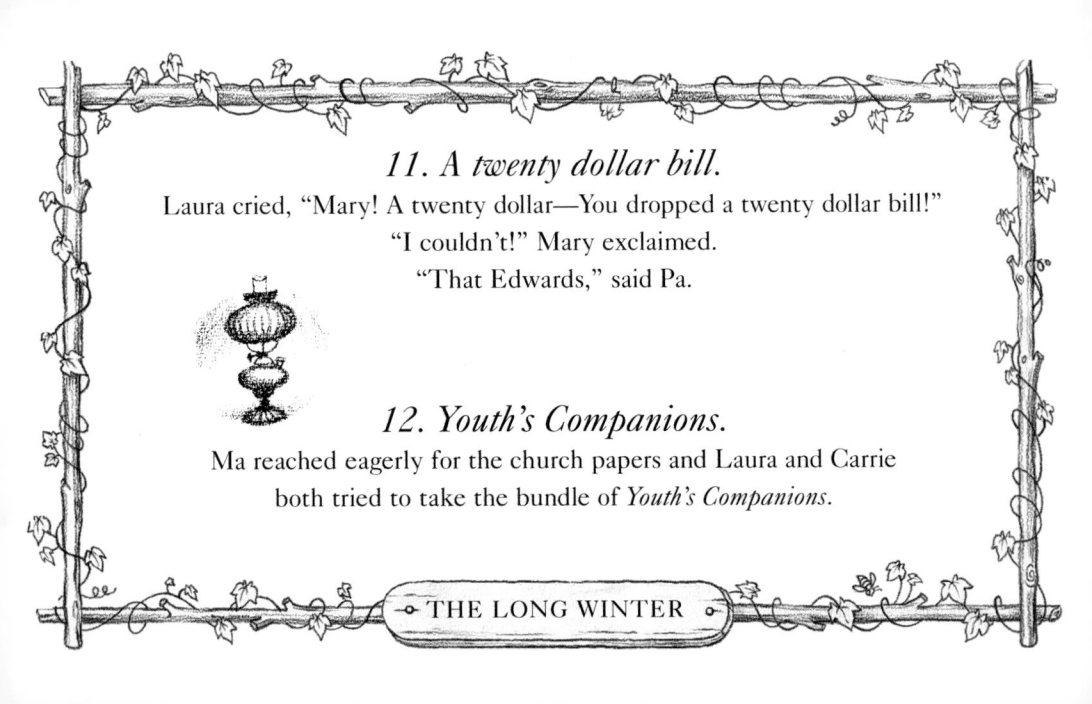

12. *Youth's Companions.*

Ma reached eagerly for the church papers and Laura and Carrie
both tried to take the bundle of *Youth's Companions.*

THE LONG WINTER

13. What does Laura give Carrie for Christmas?

14. What does Laura help Pa make after the coal runs out?

THE LONG WINTER

13. An embroidered picture frame.

While she put the tiny needle through the perforations in the cardboard and drew the fine, colored wool carefully after it, she was thinking how wistfully Carrie had looked at the beautiful thing.

She decided to give it to Carrie for Christmas.

14. Make hay sticks to burn as fuel.

All that day and all the next day, Laura helped Pa twist hay while Ma kept the fire going.

THE LONG WINTER

15. What do the Ingallses use to grind wheat?

16. How much does Mr. Loftus pay Almanzo and Cap for the seed wheat?

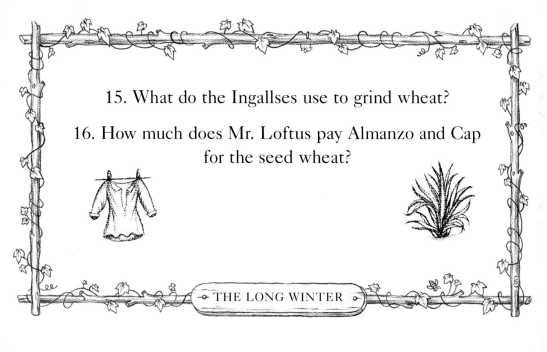

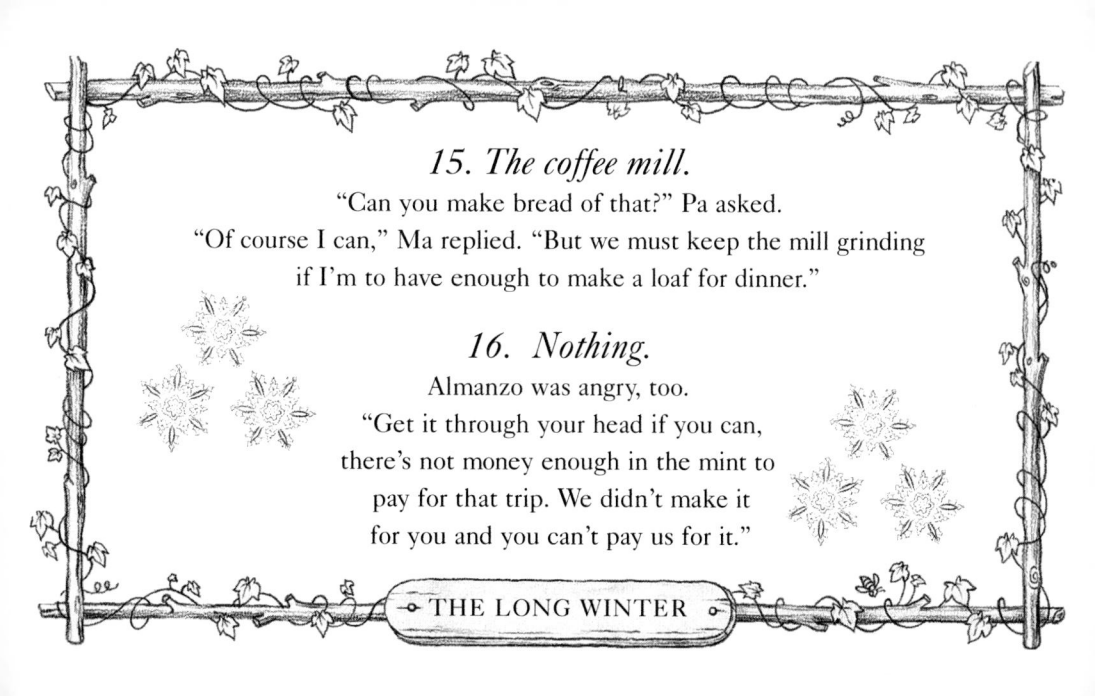

15. *The coffee mill.*

"Can you make bread of that?" Pa asked.

"Of course I can," Ma replied. "But we must keep the mill grinding
if I'm to have enough to make a loaf for dinner."

16. *Nothing.*

Almanzo was angry, too.

"Get it through your head if you can,
there's not money enough in the mint to
pay for that trip. We didn't make it
for you and you can't pay us for it."

17. What is the Chinook?

18. What is Mrs. Boast's "Christmas in May"
     present to the Ingalls family?

17. *The wind of spring.*
The Chinook, the wind of spring, was blowing.

18. *Butter.*
Laura undid the paper. There on a small plate was a ball of butter.

THE LONG WINTER

1. What eats Pa's hair in the middle of the night?

2. Who gives chickens to Ma?

LITTLE TOWN ON THE PRAIRIE

1. A mouse.

"My goodness!" Ma said weakly. "It must have been a mouse cutting off your hair to make itself a nest."

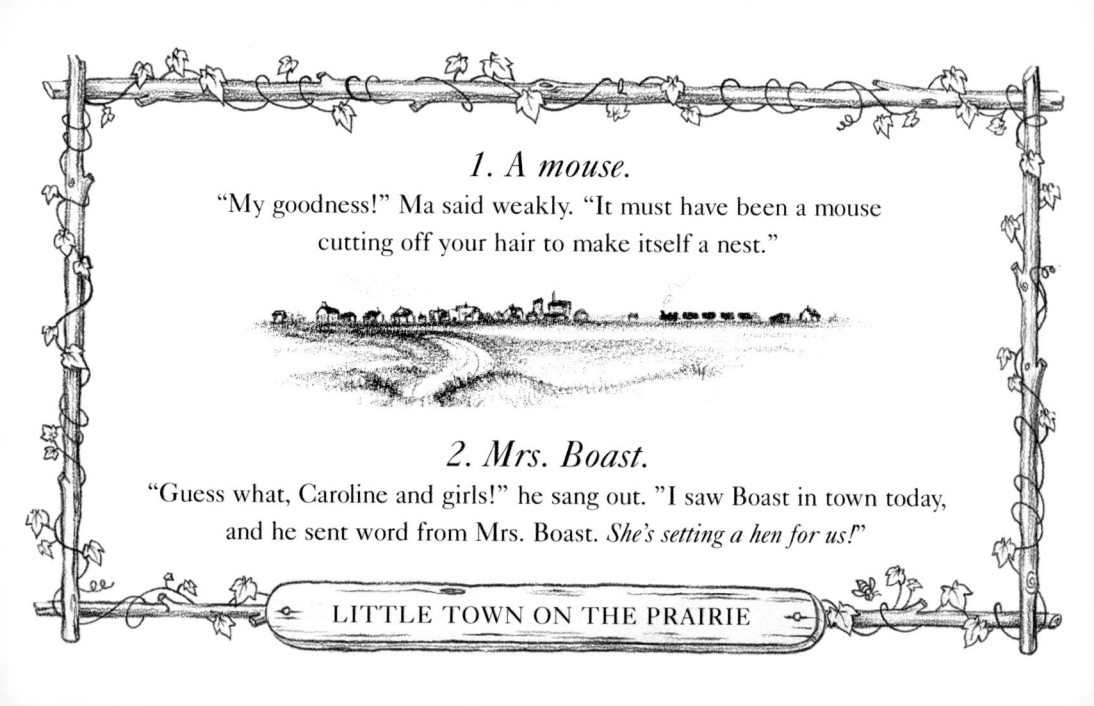

2. Mrs. Boast.

"Guess what, Caroline and girls!" he sang out. "I saw Boast in town today, and he sent word from Mrs. Boast. *She's setting a hen for us!*"

LITTLE TOWN ON THE PRAIRIE

3. Who gives Pa firecrackers on the Fourth of July?

4. How do Laura, Carrie, and Grace keep busy
   while Ma and Pa are in Iowa?

LITTLE TOWN ON THE PRAIRIE

3. Lawyer Barnes.

"Didn't cost me a cent," said Pa. "Lawyer Barnes handed them to me, said to give them to you girls."

4. They clean the house.

"Listen to me, Carrie and Grace," Laura said briskly. "We are going to clean this house from top to bottom, and we'll begin right now! So when Ma comes home, she'll find the fall housecleaning done."

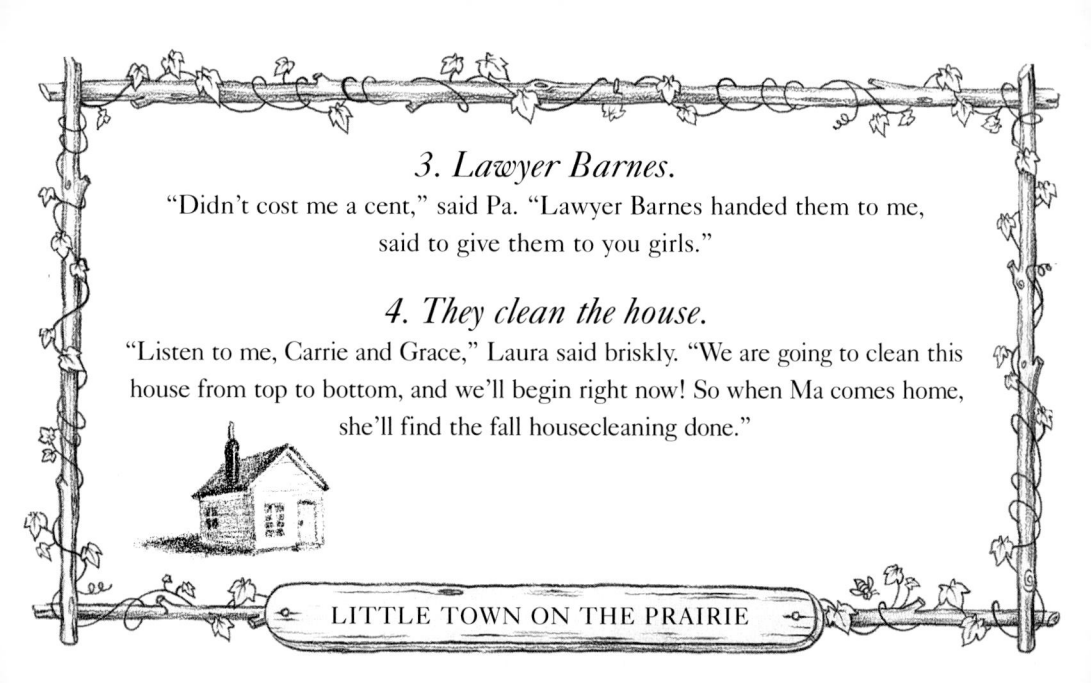

LITTLE TOWN ON THE PRAIRIE

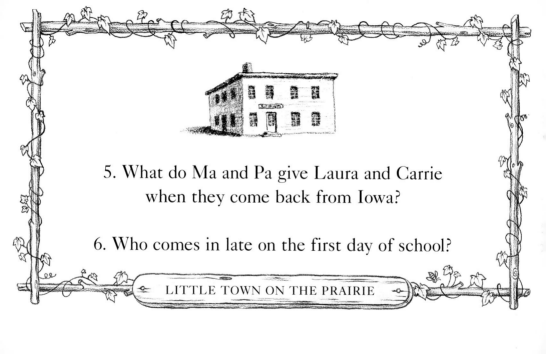

5. What do Ma and Pa give Laura and Carrie when they come back from Iowa?

6. Who comes in late on the first day of school?

LITTLE TOWN ON THE PRAIRIE

5. *Autograph albums.*

In Laura's package was a beautiful small book, too. It was thin,
and wider than it was tall. On its red cover, embossed in gold,
were the words, Autograph Album.

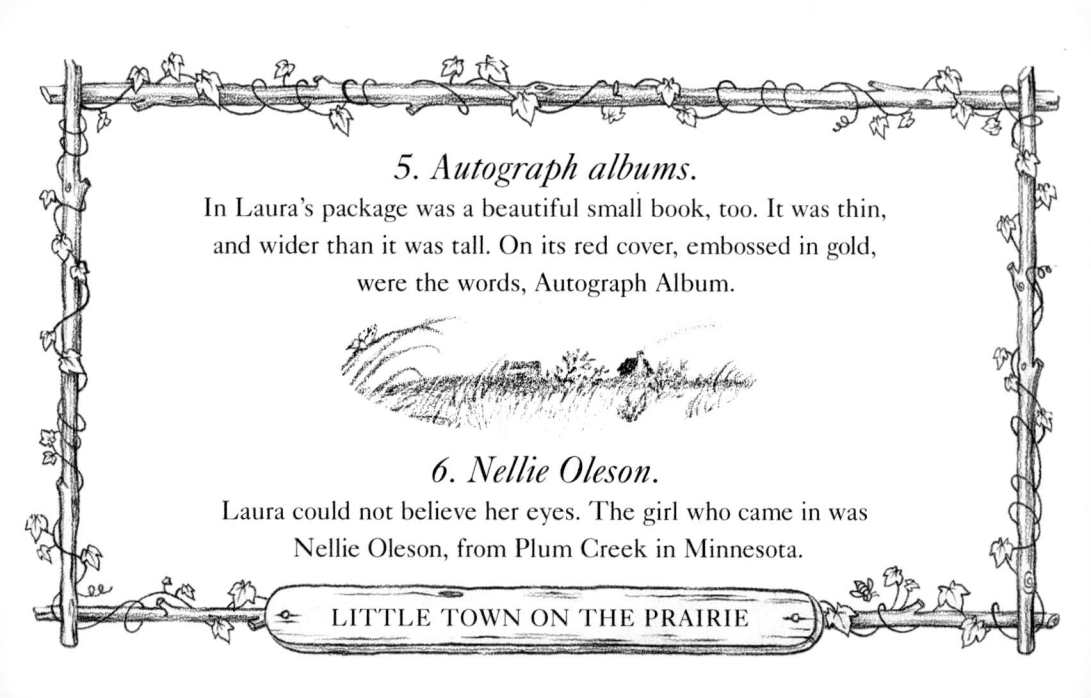

6. *Nellie Oleson.*

Laura could not believe her eyes. The girl who came in was
Nellie Oleson, from Plum Creek in Minnesota.

LITTLE TOWN ON THE PRAIRIE

7. What is the title of the book
Laura finds in Ma's bureau?

8. What is Miss Wilder's first name?

LITTLE TOWN ON THE PRAIRIE

7. *Tennyson's Poems.*

It was a perfectly new book, beautifully bound in green cloth with a gilded pattern pressed into it.

8. *Eliza Jane.*

9. What is Laura's middle name?

10. Who is the first person Laura gives a name card to?

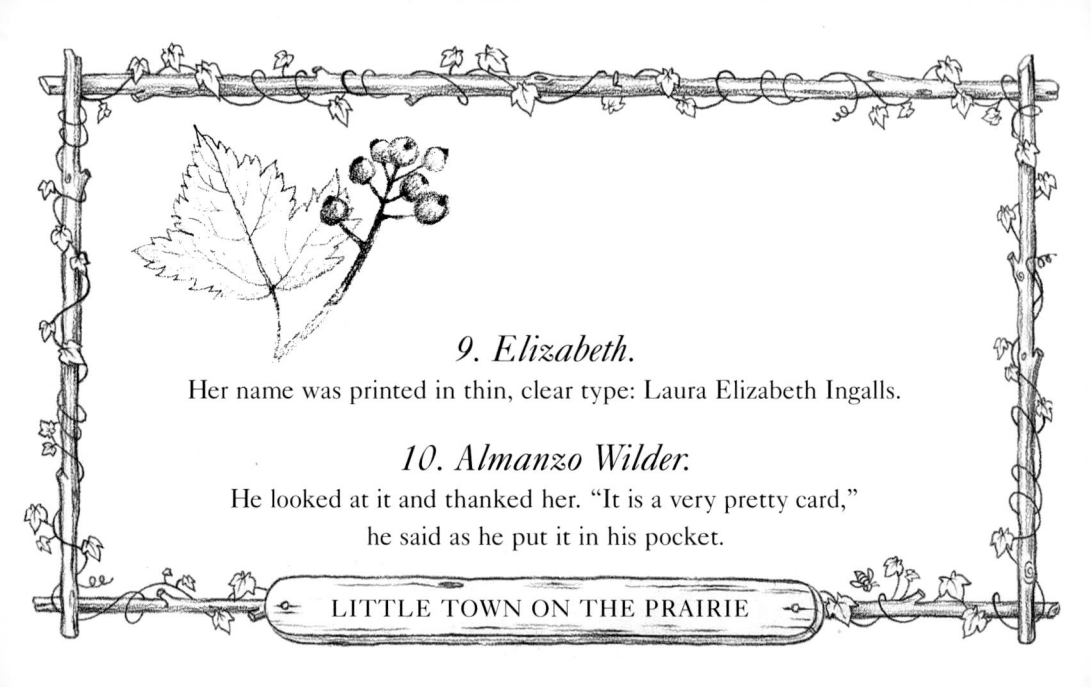

9. Elizabeth.

Her name was printed in thin, clear type: Laura Elizabeth Ingalls.

10. Almanzo Wilder.

He looked at it and thanked her. "It is a very pretty card,"
he said as he put it in his pocket.

LITTLE TOWN ON THE PRAIRIE

11. What word does Laura misspell at the literary society?

12. Who spells down the whole town?

11. *Xanthophyll.*

12. *Pa.*

There had never been such thundering applause as that applause for Pa.
He had spelled down the whole town.

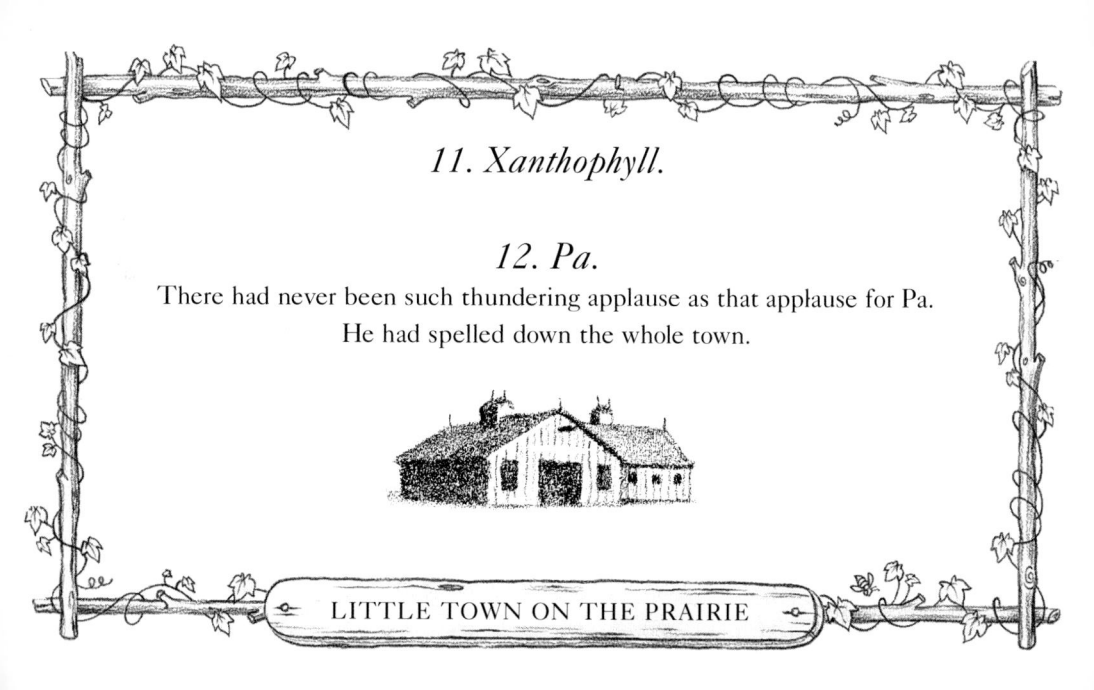

13. Who organizes the Thanksgiving celebration
at the church?

14. Whose birthday party does Laura go to?

LITTLE TOWN ON THE PRAIRIE

LITTLE TOWN ON THE PRAIRIE

15. In what subject does Laura get a final grade of 99?

16. After what kind of a meeting does Almanzo first see Laura home?

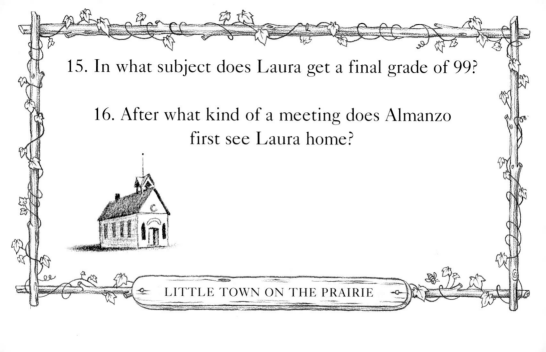

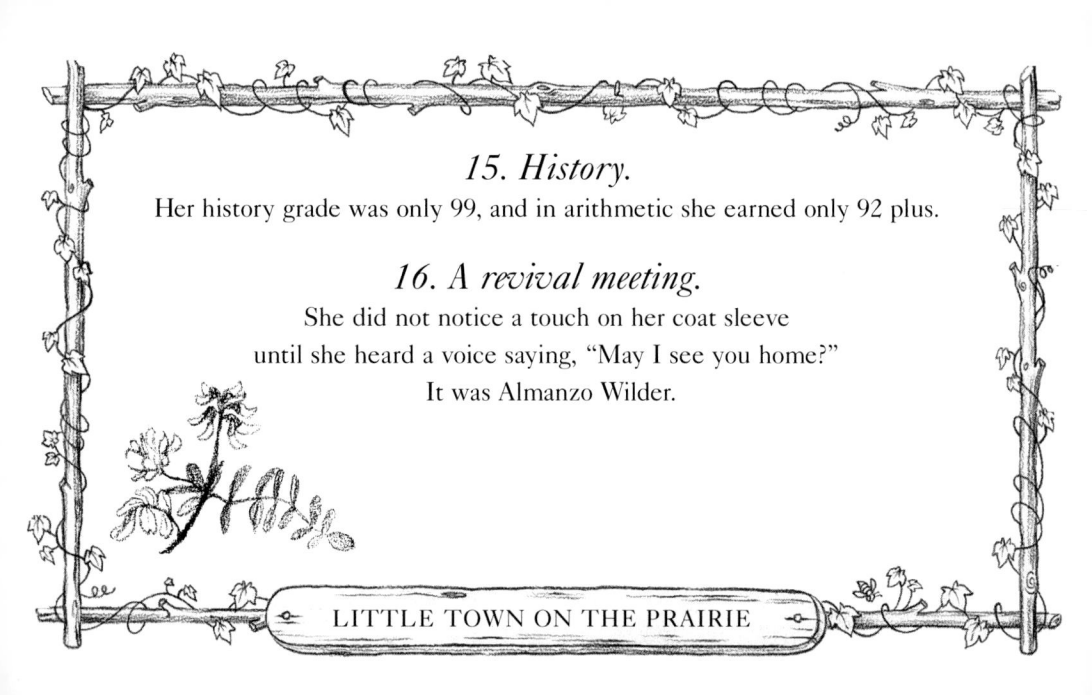

15. History.

Her history grade was only 99, and in arithmetic she earned only 92 plus.

16. A revival meeting.

She did not notice a touch on her coat sleeve
until she heard a voice saying, "May I see you home?"
It was Almanzo Wilder.

LITTLE TOWN ON THE PRAIRIE

17. What do Almanzo and Laura decide
to do together after Christmas?

18. What kind of job is offered to Laura
after the School Exhibition?

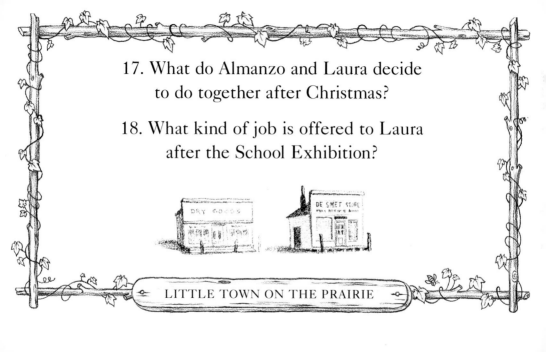

LITTLE TOWN ON THE PRAIRIE

17. *To go sleighing.*

Laura fairly danced into the house. "Oh, Pa! Ma! what do you think? Mr. Wilder's making a cutter, and he's going to take me sleighriding!"

18. *A teaching job.*

"Pa," Laura said, "I am a schoolteacher."

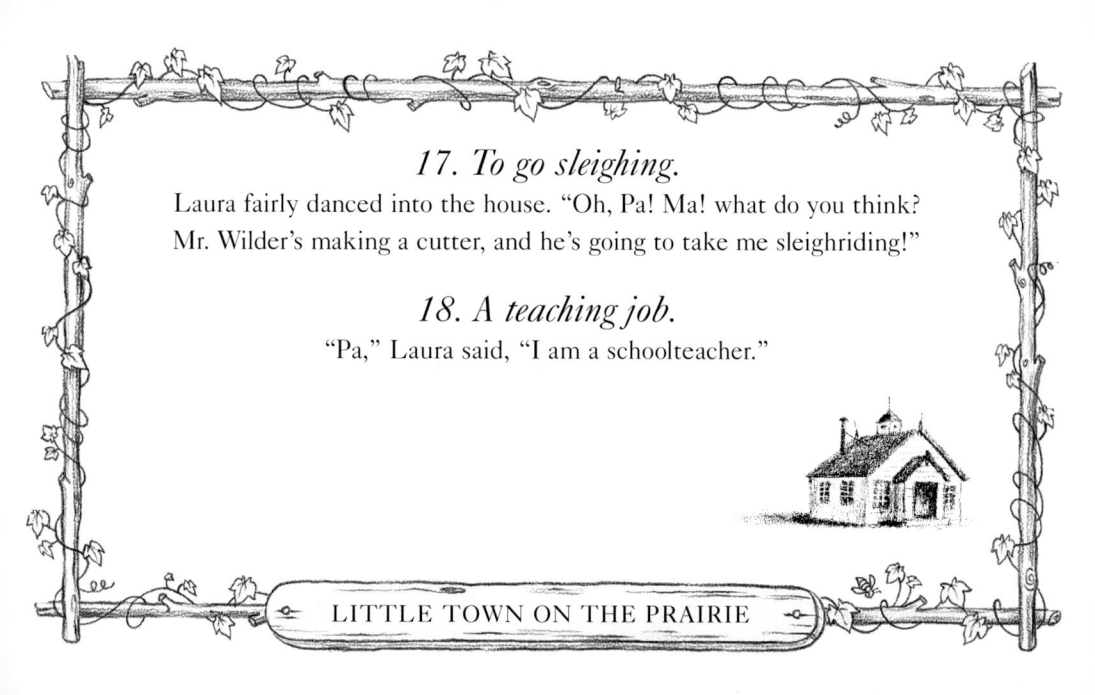

1. What are the names of Laura's students
at the Brewster school?

2. What does the Superintendent tell
Laura's students to do?

THESE HAPPY GOLDEN YEARS

1. Ruby, Tommy, and Clarence Brewster,
and Charles and Martha Harrison.

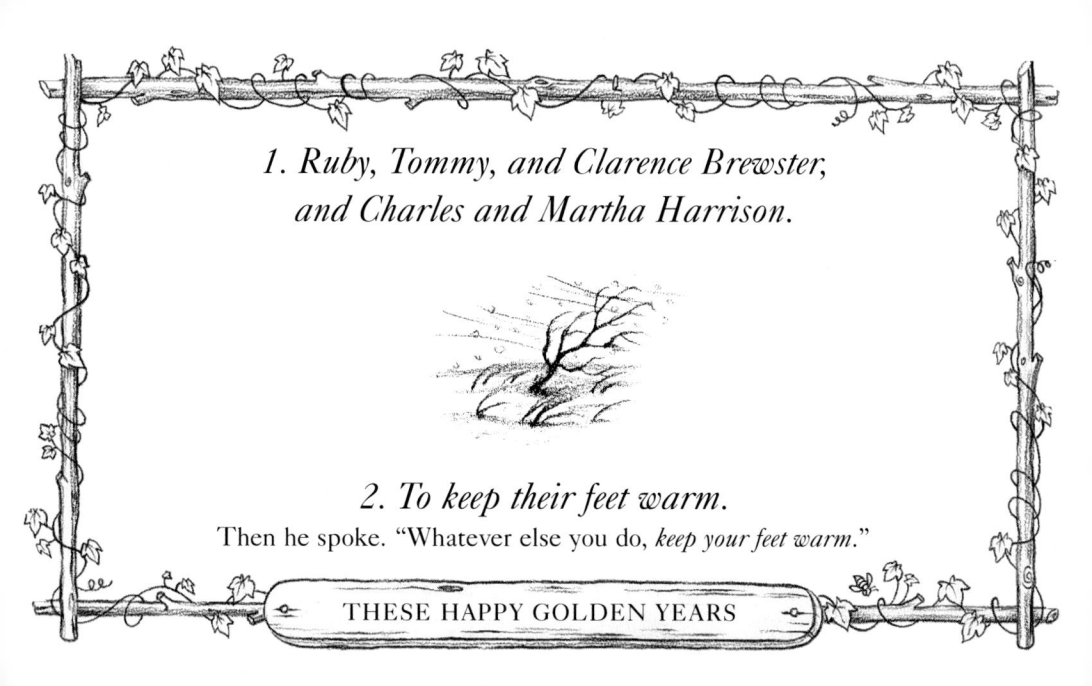

2. To keep their feet warm.
Then he spoke. "Whatever else you do, *keep your feet warm.*"

THESE HAPPY GOLDEN YEARS

3. What is the subject of Laura's first essay?

4. What relative of Laura's is Almanzo jealous of?

THESE HAPPY GOLDEN YEARS

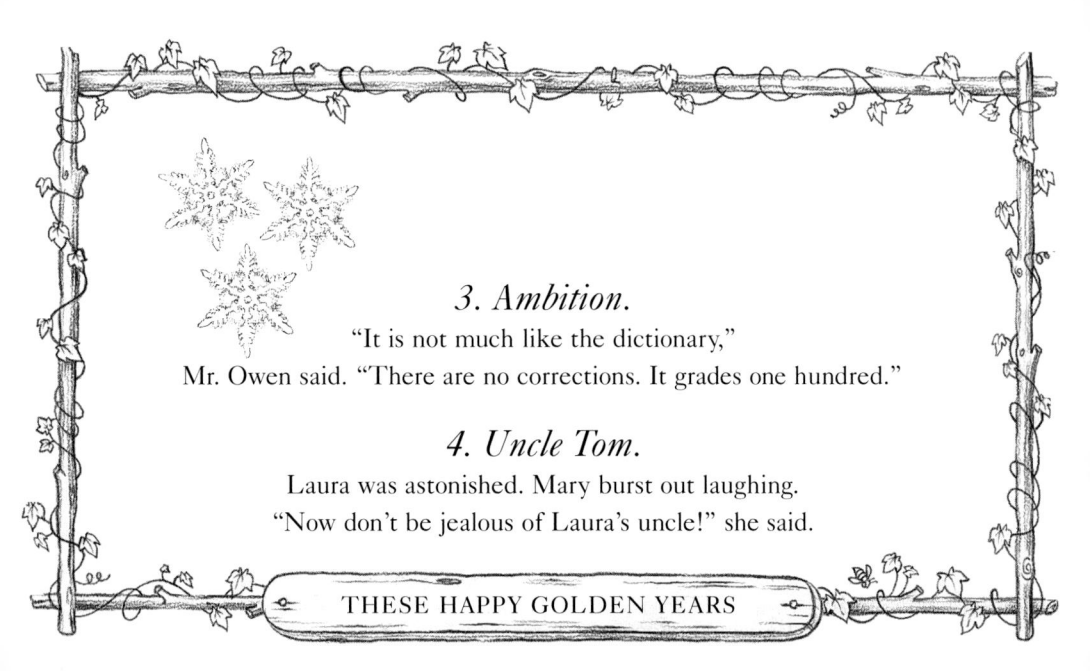

3. Ambition.

"It is not much like the dictionary,"
Mr. Owen said. "There are no corrections. It grades one hundred."

4. Uncle Tom.

Laura was astonished. Mary burst out laughing.
"Now don't be jealous of Laura's uncle!" she said.

THESE HAPPY GOLDEN YEARS

5. What jewelry does Mary bring home
   for Laura and Carrie?

6. What is the name of
   Mary's friend at college?

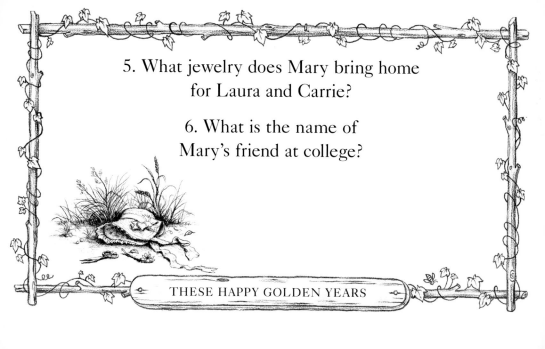

THESE HAPPY GOLDEN YEARS

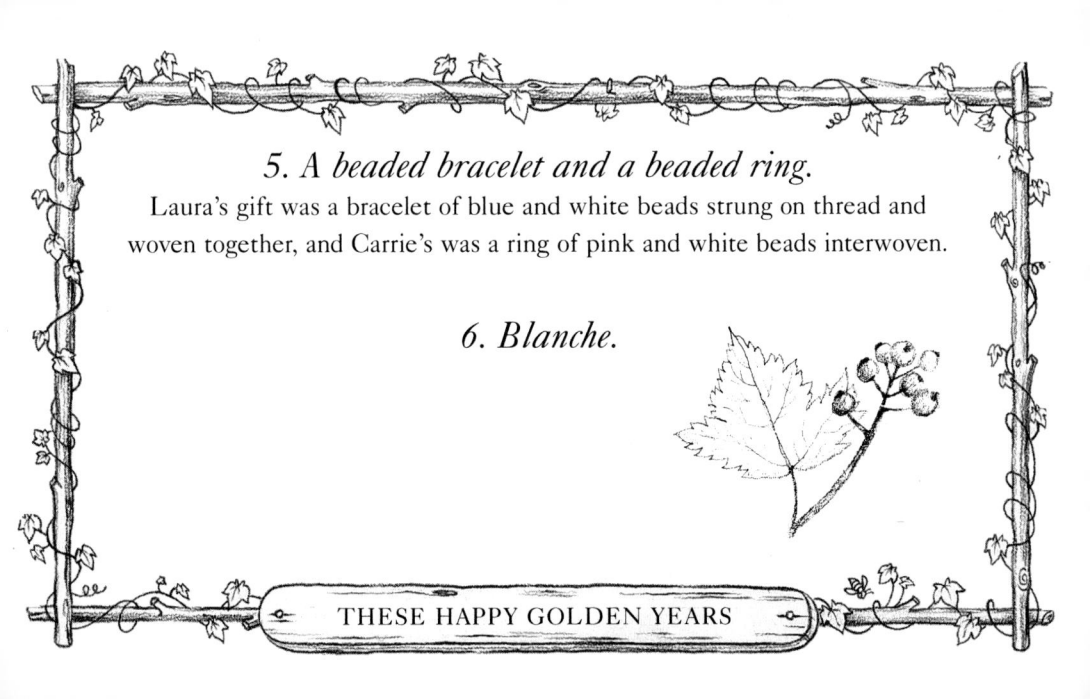

5. *A beaded bracelet and a beaded ring.*

Laura's gift was a bracelet of blue and white beads strung on thread and woven together, and Carrie's was a ring of pink and white beads interwoven.

6. *Blanche.*

7. What unexpected gift does Laura receive
at Christmas?

8. What is the name of the hills Laura and Ida
see on their Saturday walks?

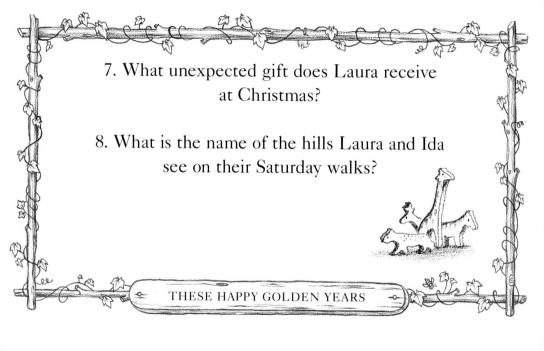

7. *A hairbrush and a comb.*

It was a small black leather case lined with blue silk.
Against the lovely blue shone, all white, an ivory-backed hairbrush and comb.

8. *The Wessington Hills.*

Laura could not say what she meant,
but to her the Wessington Hills were more than grassy hills.
Their shadowy outlines drew her with the lure of far places.

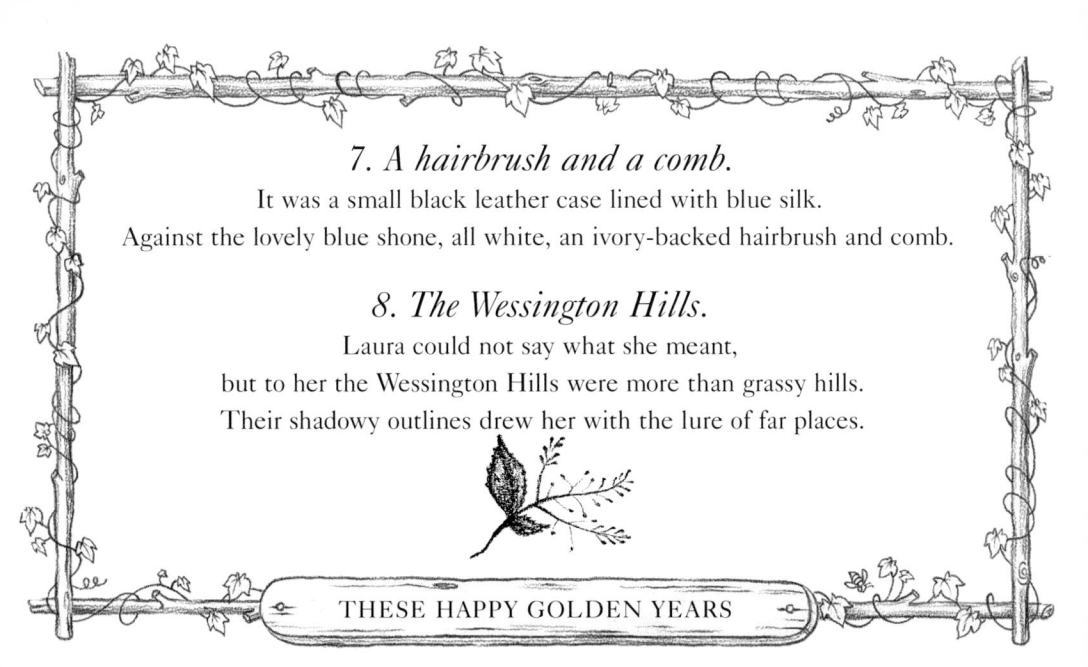

9. What is the name of the dictionary
   in the Perry school?

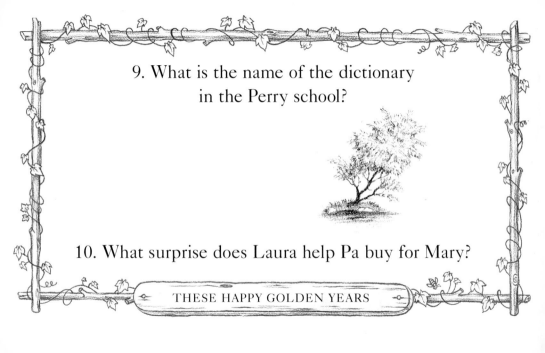

10. What surprise does Laura help Pa buy for Mary?

THESE HAPPY GOLDEN YEARS

9. Webster's Unabridged Dictionary.

The desk gleamed honey-colored in the sunlight,
and on its flat top lay a large Webster's Unabridged Dictionary.

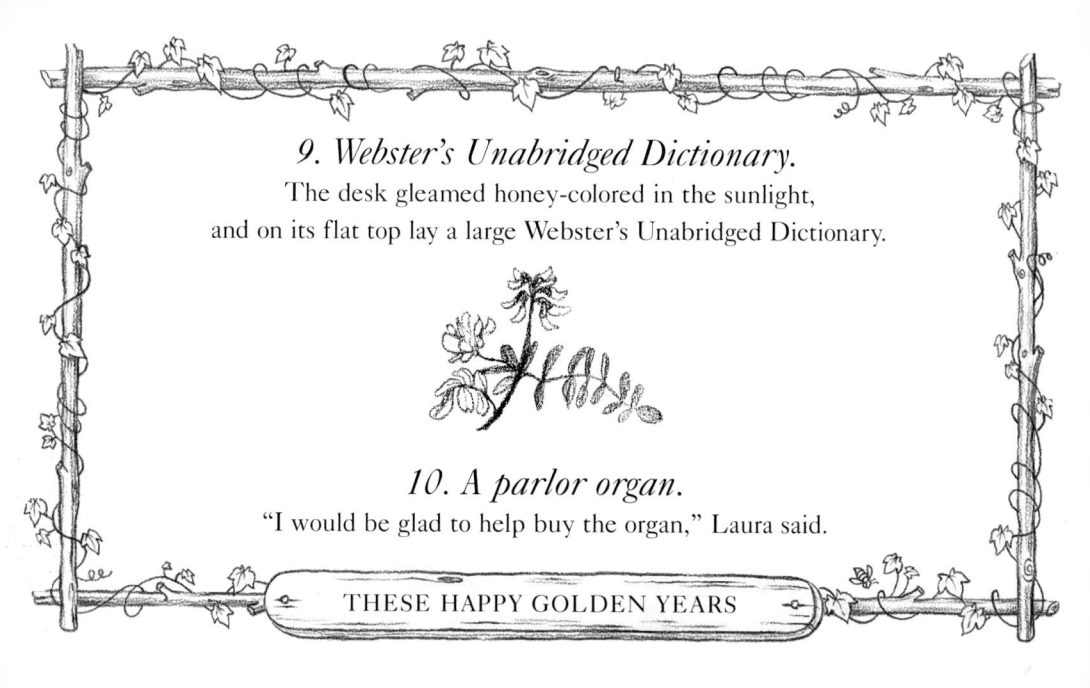

10. A parlor organ.

"I would be glad to help buy the organ," Laura said.

11. What does Nellie Oleson say
her tongue was made to do?

12. What three gems are in Laura's engagement ring?

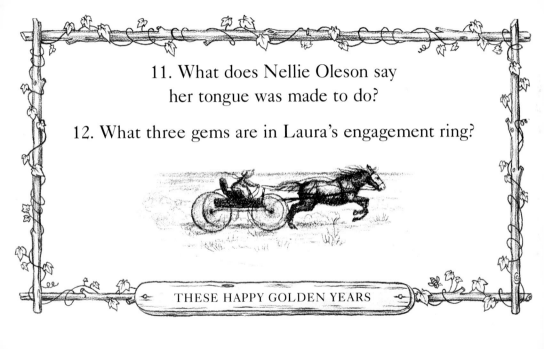

THESE HAPPY GOLDEN YEARS

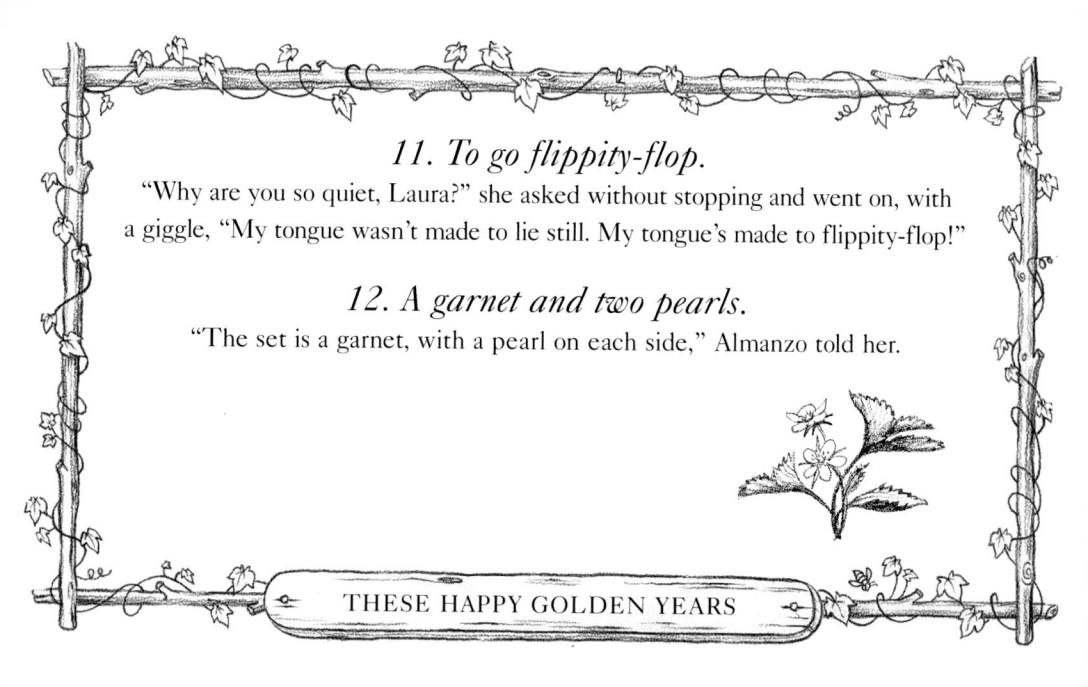

11. To go flippity-flop.

"Why are you so quiet, Laura?" she asked without stopping and went on, with a giggle, "My tongue wasn't made to lie still. My tongue's made to flippity-flop!"

12. A garnet and two pearls.

"The set is a garnet, with a pearl on each side," Almanzo told her.

THESE HAPPY GOLDEN YEARS

13. What word does Laura not want to say
as part of her wedding vows?

14. What does Pa give to Laura when she gets married?

13. Obey.

"Well, I am not going to say I will obey you," said Laura.

14. Fawn, Laura's favorite cow.

"Oh, Pa!" Laura cried. "Do you really mean I may take Fawn with me?"

"That is exactly what I do mean!" Pa said.

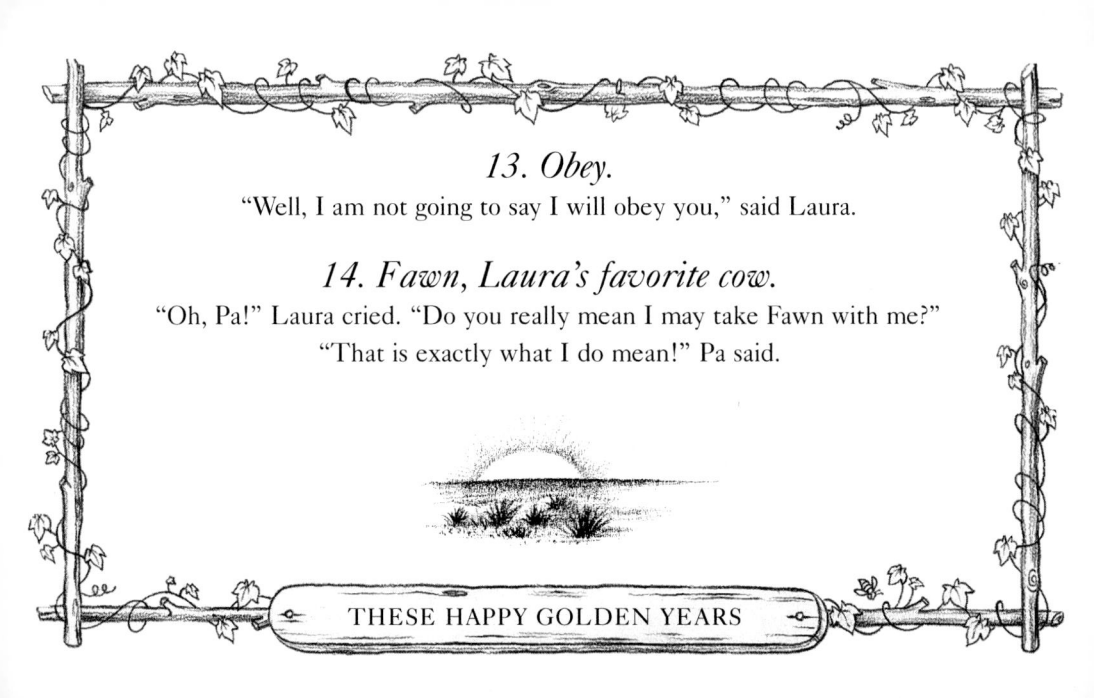

THESE HAPPY GOLDEN YEARS

15. What is the last thing Grace gives to Laura as she and Almanzo drive away?

16. Which horses bring Laura and Almanzo to their new home?

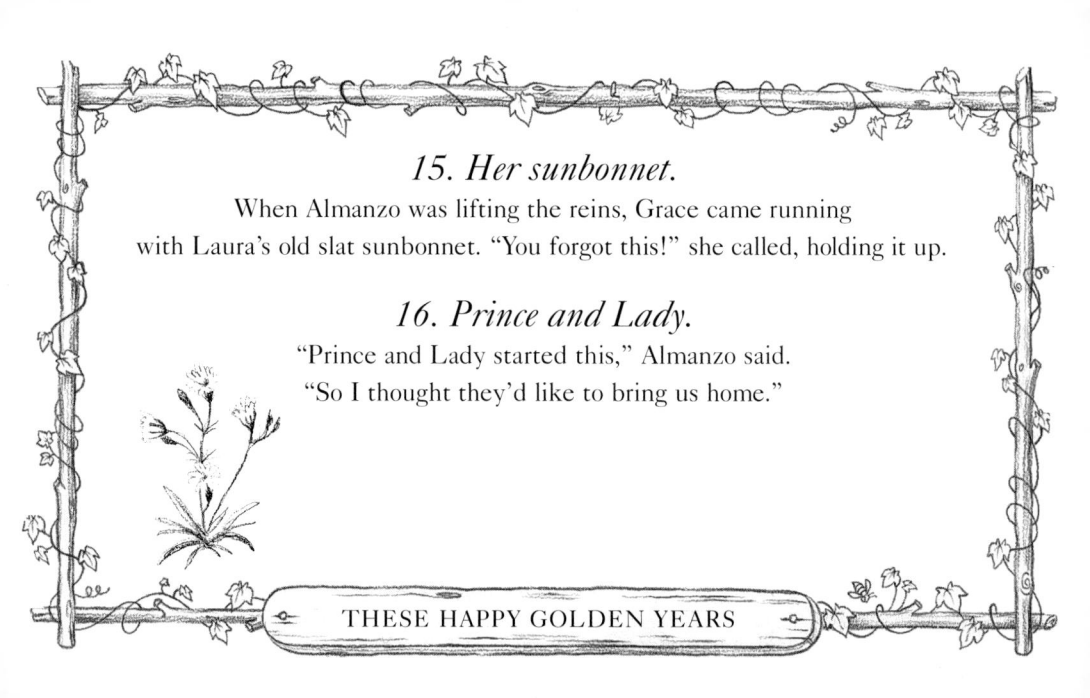

15. Her sunbonnet.

When Almanzo was lifting the reins, Grace came running
with Laura's old slat sunbonnet. "You forgot this!" she called, holding it up.

16. Prince and Lady.

"Prince and Lady started this," Almanzo said.
"So I thought they'd like to bring us home."

THESE HAPPY GOLDEN YEARS

1. Who does Laura cook her first entire dinner for?

2. What is wrong with the beans Laura cooks?

THE FIRST FOUR YEARS

1. The threshers.
It would be the first dinner in the new home
and she must cook it for the threshers!

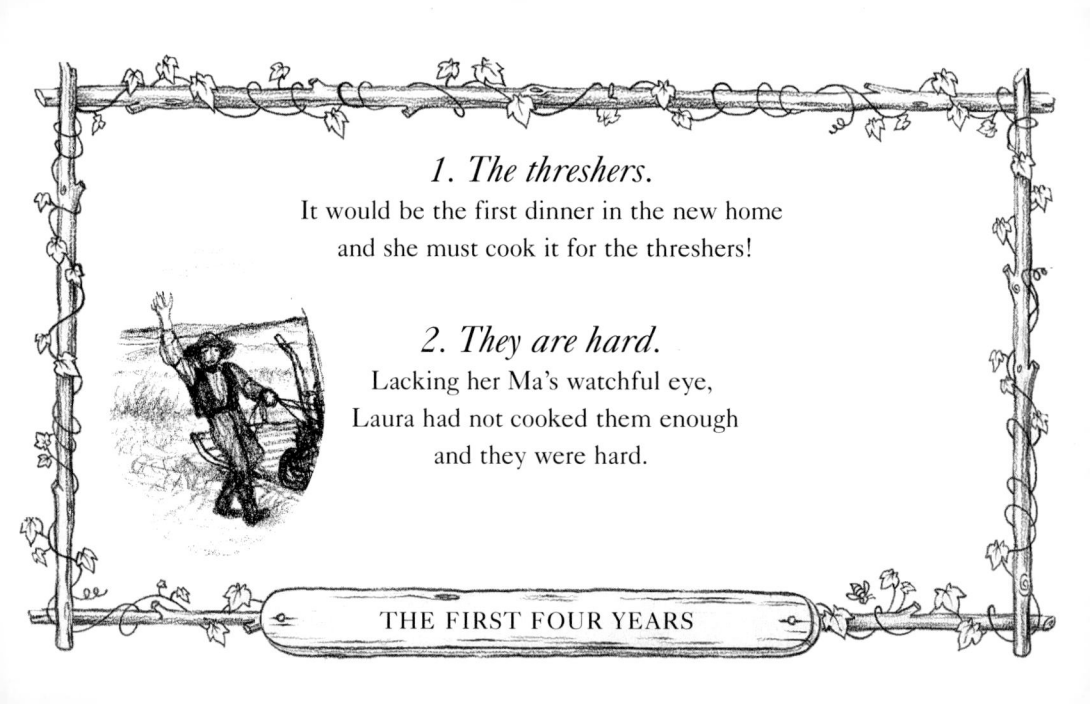

2. They are hard.
Lacking her Ma's watchful eye,
Laura had not cooked them enough
and they were hard.

THE FIRST FOUR YEARS

3. How many horses does Almanzo have to use
to break the sod?

4. What holiday do the Ingallses and the Boasts celebrate
at Laura and Almanzo's house?

THE FIRST FOUR YEARS

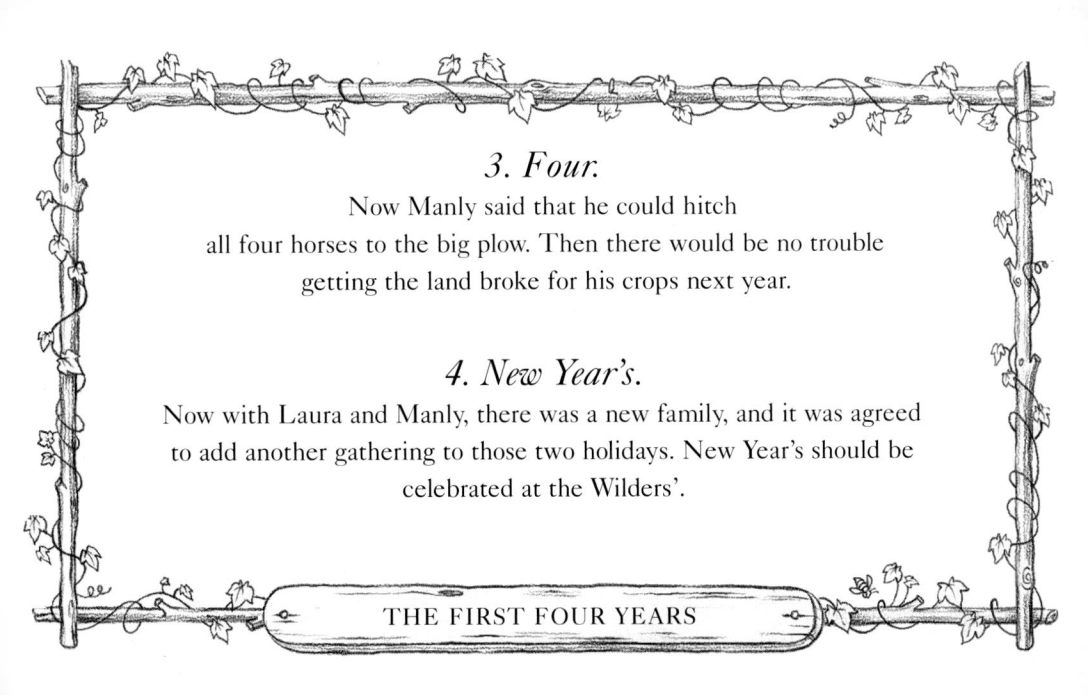

3. Four.

Now Manly said that he could hitch
all four horses to the big plow. Then there would be no trouble
getting the land broke for his crops next year.

4. New Year's.

Now with Laura and Manly, there was a new family, and it was agreed
to add another gathering to those two holidays. New Year's should be
celebrated at the Wilders'.

5. Where do Laura and Almanzo
order their Christmas present from?

6. What kind of storm ruins the first wheat crop?

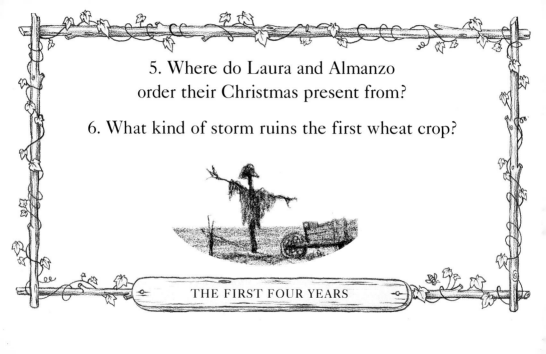

THE FIRST FOUR YEARS

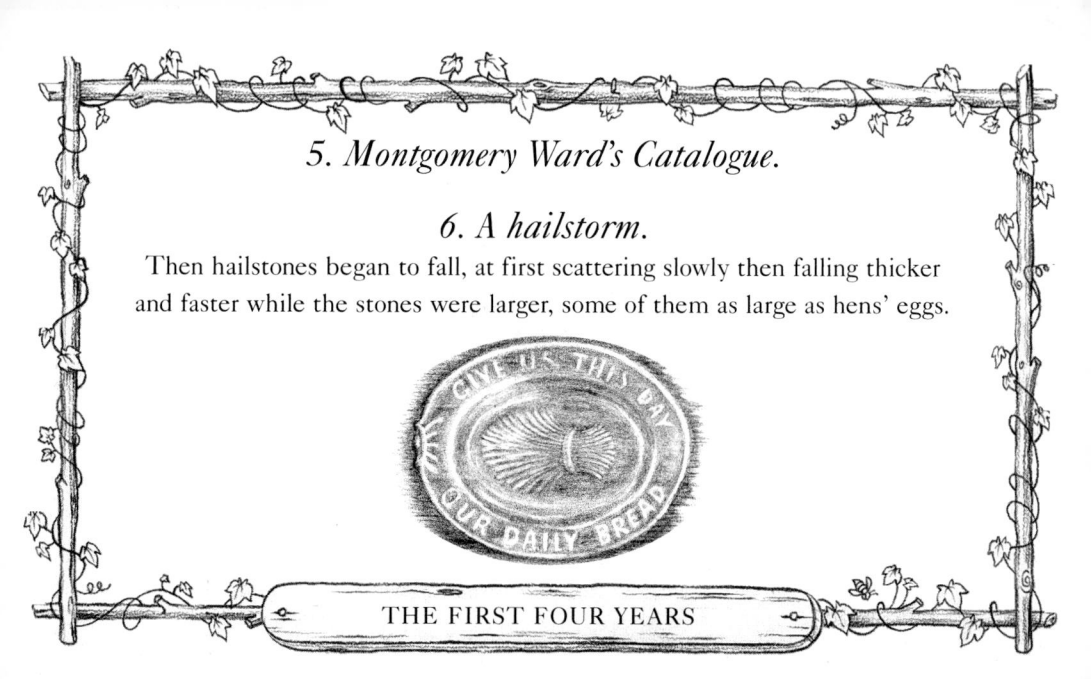

5. Montgomery Ward's Catalogue.

6. A hailstorm.

Then hailstones began to fall, at first scattering slowly then falling thicker and faster while the stones were larger, some of them as large as hens' eggs.

GIVE US THIS DAY
OUR DAILY BREAD

THE FIRST FOUR YEARS

7. How much does Rose weigh when she is born?

8. What illness do Laura and Almanzo catch?

THE FIRST FOUR YEARS

7. *Eight pounds.*

"See your little daughter, Laura! A beautiful baby
and she weighs just eight pounds," Ma said.

8. *Diptheria.*

The doctor when he came
said it was not a cold at all
but a bad case of diptheria.

9. What books does Mr. Sheldon give to Laura
when she feels ill?

10. What kind of sheep do Laura and Almanzo raise?

THE FIRST FOUR YEARS

9. Sir Walter Scott's Waverly novels.

Mr. Sheldon stepped inside, and taking the sack by the bottom, poured the contents out on the floor. It was a paper-backed set of Waverly novels.

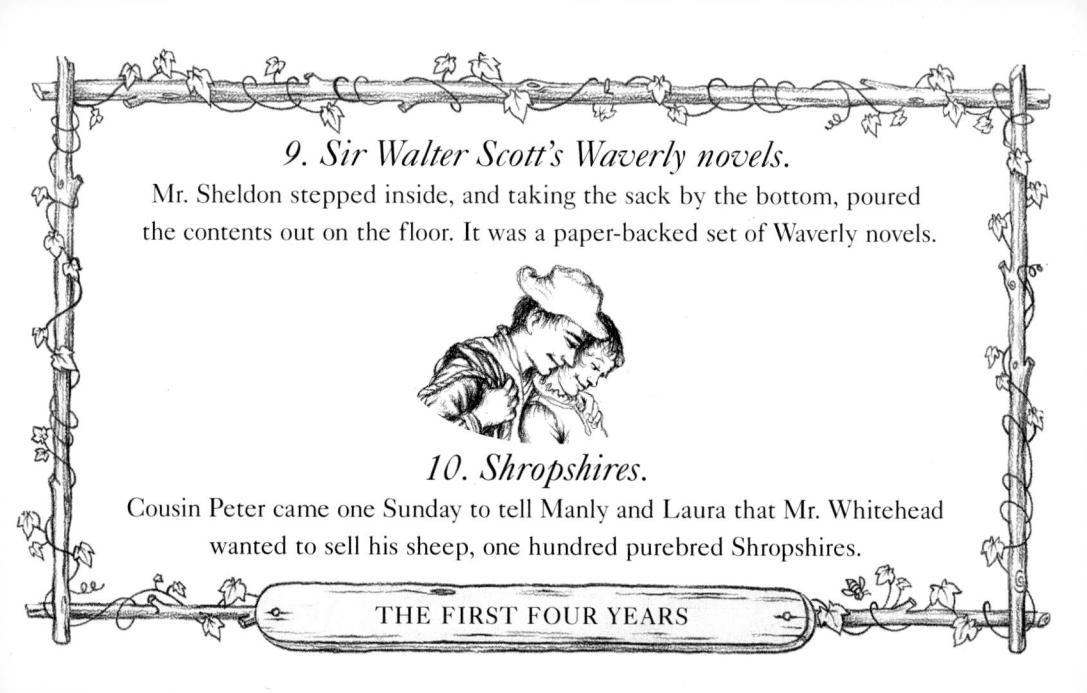

10. Shropshires.

Cousin Peter came one Sunday to tell Manly and Laura that Mr. Whitehead wanted to sell his sheep, one hundred purebred Shropshires.

THE FIRST FOUR YEARS